Local Authority Conveyancing Law and Practice

V. Charles Ward

Copyright © 2024: Vivian Charles Ward

All rights reserved.

ISBN: 979833798904

AUTHOR NOTE

The law is stated as at September 2024

CONTENTS

1	Introduction	1
2	The Added Value	5
3	Professional Rules	8
4	In-House Survival	43
5	Transaction Outline	59
6	Title Investigation	82
7	Document Drafting	116
8	Legal Resources	132
9	Development and CPO	154
10	Tax	167
	Index	177
	References	179

1 INTRODUCTION

This is not a textbook on how to do conveyancing. There is not enough room for that. In writing this book we have assumed that you know at least the mechanics of conveyancing in England and Wales. That you know how to download title information; put in searches or draft a standard-form contract, or use on-line drafting tools like Practical Law. That most of you reading this book will already be working as part of an in-house conveyancing team, whether you have already qualified, or are in the process of qualifying as a legal professional, or whether you are someone, as yet, without formal legal qualification, but who has some practical experience in working as part of an in-house conveyancing team, perhaps as a legal secretary or paralegal. But maybe you are not a lawyer at all. Perhaps you are part of your council's estates team. Or part of its housing regeneration team. Or a qualified private-practice lawyer who is thinking of going in-house.

Maybe you are not employed in-house at all. Maybe you are working for an external firm of solicitors commissioned to carry out work for a local authority client. And you need to get up to speed quickly with the special rules which apply to local authority conveyancing. Maybe you are a self-employed barrister working at a chambers specialising in real estate, who needs to quickly understand the environment in which your client-team works.

This book is intended to provide an easy source of reference for anything to do with local authority conveyancing transactions, which might otherwise require hours of Internet-research, particularly as regards such things as statutory devolution of title or the special powers which exist, which enable councils to deal with restrictive covenants, which might otherwise prove problematic for a proposed redevelopment. But it is not just a source of reference material. The book, is also packed with practical advice on how anyone can make the most of their career as part of an in-house conveyancing team. It will also encourage you to look closely at any management or promotion opportunities which may exist within your team (whether permanent or temporary) and help you to become part of your team's success story. You may be surprised to discover what is really important to any corporate client. And it's not about being 'cheap and cheerful'. It will help you navigate the bureaucracy of a local authority transaction. How to develop those key working relationships with your instructing officers which will make you the 'go to' person for any legal query or task.

At the last count, around 25% of all registered solicitors in England and Wales worked in-house. That's 26,000 practising solicitors. And they're just the ones with practising certificates. The figure could even be higher, as some qualified solicitors working for organisations may not have practising certificates, because the law does not require them to do so. We must then add to those statistics, the Chartered Legal Executives; Licensed Conveyancers; trainees and paralegals, who work alongside those solicitors.

In house lawyers work across a range of organisations, including some of the largest companies, as well as not-for-profits, such as housing associations, as well as civil service departments, local government and other public sector organisations. They are also engaged across a range of professional disciplines, including company law; litigation; human resources, intellectual property, and social services.

Whilst many large companies will employ lawyers at their head offices, for the most part, their role is 'corporate'. That is to say, that they provide key legal support to company directors and senior managers of the company for which they work, as well as associated companies, for whom they may be the first point of contact as regards any legal query.

They may sit in company board meetings. They will certainly know the company's business and have professional expertise in certain areas of the law, such as contracts, company law, human resources and intellectual property. Because these are the core legal skills for any corporate lawyer. They may also act as an interface between the company and its external lawyers. But it is rare that a public company will entrust its routine legal work, such as conveyancing or litigation, to an in-house legal team. It just wouldn't be cost effective. And it is not usually a company's core business. Such volume work would routinely be outsourced to a law firm which has both the expertise and the resource to deal with it.

But responsibility would remain with that in-house corporate counsel to manage that outsourcing and to ensure that the company's requirements are met. An exception to this way of working are the many local authority legal departments which, continue to process volume work, using a team of lawyers which they employ directly. For a local housing authority, that work might include: right-to buy sales; residential lease extensions, commercial lettings as well as complex development work.

That is not to say that these local authorities will not outsource conveyancing work to external firms of solicitors when they need to, either because they lack the internal resource to handle a particular volume of work or because they require a specific type of expertise. Currently there are an estimated 4,770 solicitors working for local authorities, only some of whom work in conveyancing.

It also cannot be assumed that all big local authorities adopt this business model for the processing of volume transactional work. There is nothing to prevent a local authority, of any size, maintaining only a corporate core of in-house lawyers and outsourcing all of their volume conveyancing and litigation to private law firms. The bottom tier of local government are the estimated 9000 town and parish councils, which, for the most part, will not directly employ any legal staff, other than, perhaps, a legally qualified clerk. Usually the small amount of any legal work which any town or parish council is able to generate, can easily be accommodated by any local firm of solicitors having the appropriate resources and expertise.

2 THE ADDED VALUE

In the mid-1980s, the directors of Unilever, the Anglo Dutch conglomerate, carried out what they termed a 'Greenfield Review' of its head office services, based at London Blackfriars. They assumed, for the purposes of this exercise, that the company was starting afresh with nothing more than a greenfield, and carried out a detailed assessment of what a company like Unilever, starting from scratch, would require in terms of head office services and how those services should be provided.

It meant that every head office team had to justify its existence as part of the in-house function, including legal and surveying services. As it was, Unilever's tiny in-house conveyancing team survived the review intact, whilst its larger surveying team, which had traded under the name of Kirkwood Craig & Partners, was reduced to a rump. It resulted in a series of forced redundancies, as those volume surveying functions were outsourced to other firms, together with those of the staff who were lucky enough to transfer to those outsourced jobs.

It was the same exercise which larger councils in England and Wales were required to carry out a decade later as a result of a government programme of compulsory competitive tendering, which meant that those councils were only allowed keep legal and other professional services in-house if those services had previously been put out to tender and other prospective suppliers had been given an opportunity to bid for the work.

If the in-house team wished to retain the work, it had to formulate its own bid, in response to the tender, which would then be evaluated alongside every competing private sector bid for the same work. The council's elected members would then be required to decide which of the bids were the most economically advantageous and allocate the work accordingly.

The consequence of compulsory competitive tendering was that many volume legal services, including notably conveyancing, which had previously been undertaken by an in-house legal team, was now outsourced to those private firms of solicitors which had been successful in their bids.

Following a change of government in 1997, compulsory competitive tendering was abolished and replaced by the softer Duty of Best Value, in which there is still an expectation that in-house professional services will be outsourced where it is cost effective to do so.

What we have now, in most larger local authorities, is a mixed economy, in which some volume legal work is outsourced, with other work being kept in-house. There is also the hybrid situation, where professional services of any type can be outsourced to a shared service organisation, hosted by one of the local authorities but in which all the participating local authorities have a stake. Which brings us to our fundamental question: "What is the point of an in-house legal service?".

It's About the Added Value

The answer to that question has to be the added-value which any in-house professional service can provide to an organisation, above that of an outsourced service. That in turn begs further questions. What is the added-value that an in-house professional service can provide? And why is it so important? Here is a clue.

It is <u>not</u> about price. Nobody cares that you only charge out at £89 per hour compared to the £220 per hour which a corporate client might routinely expect to pay to a commercial firm for the same work. What is really important to a corporate client is the quality of the service, the expertise and speed of turnaround. And most corporate clients are prepared to pay more for that quality of service.

They want someone who can take the burden from their shoulders. Someone who doesn't have to be chased. Someone who gets on with the work and delivers the desired result.

A phrase we often hear repeated is 'managing expectations'. It can provide an excuse for poor service. No corporate client wants their expectations 'managed'. Their expectations are what they are. If that person is to be kept as a client, those expectations have to be accommodated.

The worst thing which you can say to a corporate client is that you have been too busy to deal with their work and are not able to guarantee a realistic deadline for getting it completed. Many clients will just take their work elsewhere. You will have lost them forever.

So what can an in-house professional service offer by way of 'added-value'. Here are some suggestions:

1. **The value of having someone on-site who knows the client's business** and who is able to deal with client-queries quickly and as they arise without the paraphernalia of a formal instruction and a bill at the end. Even if you are working from home, you can still be reached on a teams call or by telephone.
2. **The value of someone who can work as a team with the other in-house professionals.**
3. **The value of having someone on board who can deal with the administrative matters associated with a local authority transaction, which would not routinely be undertaken by an external lawyer.** Examples would include preparation of cabinet or delegated reports and decisions needed to get constitutional authority for an exchange of contracts or completion of a transaction. Making a presentation to councillors or other chief officers. Only you can do that.
4. **Miscellaneous local authority tasks not related to any specific transaction but which requires some conveyancing knowledge.** Examples might include, responding to a freedom of information request. Or dealing with an application to register a property as an asset of community value under the Localism Act 2011.
5. **Someone who can keep their clients updated on changes in the law or other legal developments which affect their work.**

3 PROFESSIONAL RULES

In this chapter we look at the specific professional issues relating to the way a local authority conveyancer carries out their work, whether you are on the payroll of the particular local authority for whom you carry out work or whether you are engaged through an agency on a locum contract or simply working freelance.

A feature of many public sector organizations is the high turnover of staff. A reason for this is the limited opportunities for internal promotion, because of the way public sector recruitment is structured. The result is a steady movement of staff between local authorities, as individual employees look for promotion or better terms and conditions. That, coupled with the amount of internal resource required to fill permanent posts, means that many local authorities rely on the agency staff to fill vacancies quickly without the need to go through a longwinded recruitment process. However, whatever the terms of engagement, all qualified legal staff providing services exclusively to their local authority, work within the same regulatory framework.

Our starting point for this chapter has to be the following three documents, one of which is published by the Solicitors Regulation Authority (SRA), and the remaining two by the Law Society, and which are freely downloadable from the Internet. Those documents are:

1. Rule 4 (In-House Practice) of the SRA Standards and Regulations, published 25 November, 2019, which replaced by the 2011 SRA Handbook;
2. Law Society Practice Note, 'Solicitors offering Legal Services to the Public From Unregulated Entities.'
3. Law Society Practice Note 'In-House Practice: Regulatory Requirements, published 1 September, 2022;

We focus only on those parts of that regulatory guidance which is most relevant to solicitors and other professional legal staff working in-house for a local authority. A local authority is deemed an 'unregulated entity' as they are not an 'authorised body' as defined by the SRA standards and regulations, which is defined to mean a law firm authorised by the SRA. With some exceptions, which are explained below, in-house solicitors are restricted to advising the organisation they work for. As regards solicitors working in-house for a local government organisation, the rules are set out in Rule 4 of the SRA Standards and Regulations, the relevant parts of which is set out below, together with further explanation where required.

The General Position

The default position is that in-house solicitors work on the same professional rules as their private sector counterparts. That is to say that you, as a qualified solicitor, must act:

- In a way that upholds the constitutional principle of the rule of law and the proper administration of justice;
- In a way that uphold public trust and confidence in the solicitors' profession and in legal services provided by authorised persons;
- With independence;
- With integrity;
- In the best interests of its clients.

Working in-house for a local authority generally means working only for your employer and other associated organisations, including subsidiary companies, as well as other public sector organisations for whom your local authority is authorised by statute to provide goods and services.

Do I need a solicitors Practising Certificate if I am working in-house for local authority?

Whether you need a solicitor's practising certificate whilst working in-house depends either on the type of work which you do or whether you hold yourself out as a solicitor in your dealings with other people, including other legal professionals. It is a combination of factors.

You will need a solicitors practising certificate, firstly if you are involved in legal practice; and secondly, if any of the following criteria apply:

- Your work depends on you being a solicitor;
- You work with others who regard you as a solicitor and rely on your undertakings, confidentiality, and so on;
- You are held out explicitly or implicitly as a practising solicitor;
- You are employed explicitly or implicitly as a solicitor;
- That you are required to undertake or supervise the provision of reserved legal activities as part of your role, or
- You are deemed by section1A of the Solicitors Act 1974 to be acting as a solicitor (see below).

In relation to the last, Section 1A of the Solicitors Act 1974, introduced by later legislation and headed, **"Practising Certificates: Employed Solicitors**, states:

"A person who has been admitted as a solicitor and whose name is on the roll shall, if he would not otherwise be taken to the acting as a solicitor, be taken for the purposes of this Act to be so acting if he is employed in connection with the provision of legal services:

a) by any person who is qualified to act as a solicitor;
b) by any partnership at least one member of which is so qualified;
c) By any body recognized under Section 9 of the Administration of Justice Act 1985 (incorporated practices); or
d) by any other person who, for the purposes of the Legal Services Act 2007, is an authorised person in relation to an activity which is a reserved legal activity within the meaning of the Act.

It is clear from the above, that not everyone who holds a solicitor-qualification requires a solicitor's practising certificate. It depends entirely on whether they are engaged in legal work (either at an operational or supervisory level), or if they are not so engaged, whether they hold themselves out as being a solicitor or require that qualification as a term of their employment.

It is not uncommon to see qualified solicitors not engaged in legal work, referring to themselves as 'non-practising' or not referring to the qualification at all. If your work involves hands-on conveyancing (either in an operational or a supervisory role) and you are already qualified as a solicitor, it is almost certain that you will require a solicitor's practising certificate to do your work.

Even if you are in doubt as to whether you technically require a solicitors practicing certificate, it is s always better to err on the side of caution and obtain that practising certificates, even if the others in your team have chosen not to. At around £330 for the year, at the time of writing, the cost of a solicitor's practising certificate is not prohibitive and even that can be set off against tax as being a necessary expense of your employment.

Practising certificates have to be applied for online during October in every year and take effect from 1 November in each year. Applying on-line for a solicitors practising certificate is a self-certification click-through a process in which you confirm your eligibility to apply for that certificate and that you have complied with your continuous professional development obligations.

Whilst many local authorities will, as a matter of course, pay the practising certificate fees of their permanent staff, it is the personal responsibility of every practising solicitor to ensure that they have the required practising certificate which enables them to do their work.

The fact that historically the local authority has paid those fees for its permanent legal staff, provides no obligation on it to do so in the future. The expectation is also that agency solicitors contracted to the local authority to which they provide services, will be responsible for applying for their own practising certificates and, where necessary, to provide evidence that this is in place.

By obtaining a solicitors practicing certificate you are also telling the world that you are qualified to do your work and your professional details will be instantly available to anyone carrying out a search of the 'find a solicitor' website

Who is your client?

As an in-house conveyancer, your primary client is your own employer or, if you are an agency solicitor, the organisation to which you are contracted to provide services as part of their in-house team. But your employer may not only by your only client.

Your employing local authority may have subsidiary corporate interests in registered companies or limited liability partnerships in which it has a controlling interest. It may also have corporate trustee functions, which are constitutionally separate from its functions as a local authority. It may share some constitutional functions with other local authorities, such as a joint-cemetery committee, on which several local authorities are represented. Finally, there is the ability for local authorities to provide legal services to other local authorities under the Local Authorities (Goods and Services) Act 1970.

This could include the ability to act for any of the thousands of town and parish councils which exist in the UK alongside the approximately 400 district, borough, county and unitary authorities. The past 20 years is also seen the growth of shared back-office services between local authorities, including legal services, to achieve economies of scale.

Organisations to which the employing local authority is empowered by statute to provide legal services.

Local Government Act 1972 – Section 101(1) (Arrangements for the discharge of functions by local authorities) sets out the general principle, that a local authority may arrange for the discharge of their functions:(a) by a committee, a sub- committee or an officer of the local authority, or(b) by any other local authority.

Under the heading (Supply of goods and services by local authorities) Section 1 of the Local Authorities (Goods and Services) Act 1970 states:

(1) Subject to the provisions of this section, a local authority and any public body within the meaning of this section may enter into an agreement for all or any of the following purposes, that is to say:

a) the supply by the authority to the body of any goods or materials;

b) the provision by the authority of any administrative, professional or technical services;

c) the use by the body of any vehicle, plant or apparatus belonging to the authority and without prejudice to paragraph (b) above, the placing at the disposal of the body of the services of any person employed in connection with the vehicle or other property in question;or

d) the carrying out by the authority of works of maintenance in connection with the land or buildings for the maintenance of which the body is responsible.

And a local authority may purchase and store any goods on materials which in their opinion they may require for the purposes of paragraph (a) of this subsection.

(2) Nothing in paragraphs (a) to (c) of the preceding subsection authorises a local authority:

(a) to construct any building or works;

(b) to be supplied with any property or provided with any service except for the

purposes of functions conferred on the authority otherwise than by this Act.

(3) Any agreement made in pursuance of subsection one of this section may contain such terms as to payment or otherwise as the parties consider appropriate.

The remainder of the 1970 Act defines those local authorities and associated organisations which are entitled to provide goods and services to other public bodies under the Act, which in the main part are counties, districts and unitary authorities - and also defines those 'bodies' which are entitled to receive goods and services under the Act and which are defined to include even the smallest towns and parishes .

In fact so wide is the 1970 Act, that, if authorised to do so, a local authority conveyancer could act for any local authority, including the smallest town or parish council, in England or Wales.

As well as those organisations specifically defined in a of the Act as 'public bodies', to which goods and services can be supplied by a local authority provider, Section 1(5) of the Act also enables the Secretary of state, by statutory instrument, to add to the list of public bodies to which goods and services can be provided.

Several such orders have been made over the years, under the title Local Authorities (Goods and Services)(Public Bodies) Order, extending its provisions to other organisations exercising quasi-public functions, as well as other listed independent not-for-profit organisations including certain schools, hospitals and other community groups. In fact, you may be surprised by the large number of different types of organisation for whom you are authorised to act. A full list of these organisations can be found in Practical Law.

The past 20 years has also seen the growth of a new type of legal entity, the shared legal service, in which a single group of lawyers provide services to several local authorities and thereby achieve economies of scale as well as expanding the scope of resources and expertise which can be offered.

The shared service will be hosted by one of the local authorities, which will employ the legal personal and then make that resource available to the other local authorities who share use of the service on agreed terms and conditions. Again, it is the Local Authorities (Goods and Services) Act 1970, which makes such arrangements possible.

Elected Members

In most cases, the members of a local authority act corporately. Whilst each will have an individual vote, the decision made is, for constitutional purposes, the decision of the particular cabinet or committee or full council, as the case may be. But there may be circumstances when an elected member of a local authority has to act and make decisions in a personal (but public) capacity, Such as where they are the named trustee of a charity in which the council has involvement, and to which they have been nominated democratically for that purpose.

Companies

You can act for a company in which your local authority employer has a stake, either as a shareholder or as a guarantor (in the case of a company limited by guarantee). It does not have to be a controlling interest.

Even if the local authority is not a shareholder or guarantor as such, the ability to act for the company would still apply if you or an officer of your local authority, is appointed by the local authority as an officer of the company.

Legislation relevant to local authority companies includes:

* **Local Government and Housing Act 1989 Part V** - (companies in which local authorities have interests), which is the first legislation giving official recognition to the concept of the local authority company. Part V categorises local authority companies as controlled companies (in which the local authority has a controlling interest); influenced companies, (in which the local authority has at least a 15% stake); and arms-length companies, in which the local authority has less than a 15% stake.

* **The Local Authorities (Companies) Order 1995**, which further categorises local authority influenced companies as either private sector led or public sector led, depending on the amount of control exercised by the local authority. The Companies Order also requires the accounts of the company to be aggregated together with the local authority's own accounts. It also introduces other provisions to identify a company as public sector led.

* **The Local Government Act 1993 and the Localism Act 2011**, both of which give local authorities express powers to trade in function related activities but only through a limited company.

Note: that the power of a local authority conveyancer to act for subsidiary organisations is only expressed to relate to companies limited by shares or guarantee. There are no express exceptions for other incorporated organisations such as limited liability partnerships or registered societies. However, our view is that there should be no issue in an in-house solicitor acting for an LLP where the named partners are 100% controlled by the local authority.

A due diligence search of the Company's House website will suffice to confirm whether or not your employing local authority has a controlling interest in a particular company, in which case the exemption will always apply. Where the local authority's control is less than 100%, some further investigation may be required before you can be confident that you are able to act for that organisation in your in-house capacity.

Lenders

A local authority cannot mortgage its own assets. However, a local authority conveyancer may sometimes be required to deal with a property owned by a third party which is already in mortgage to the local authority, in circumstances where the owner wishes to remortgage to a different lender.

In those cases the local authority conveyancer can act for the other lender in connection with the redemption of the existing mortgage in favour of the local authority. The only qualification is that the borrowers must first be given the opportunity to be independently advised by a qualified conveyance of their choice.

Situations may arise where a local authority conveyancer has to deal with properties which are already in mortgage, possibly where the local authority is acting as a trustee for a third party in relation to a property which is in mortgage such as a deputyship sale (see below).

Sometimes a local authority conveyancer may be required to act for a local authority client, as mortgagee, where it is enforcing a statutory charge, perhaps incurred as a result of default works carried out pursuant to environmental legislation, where that default-cost has been registered as a local land charge against the property. In such cases, the local authority creditor may have the same powers of recovery as if it held a charge by way of legal mortgage.

Charities and Voluntary Organisations

Reference has already been made to the situation where a local authority does not act corporately on its own account but as trustee of a charity.

Although that charity would be constitutionally separate from the exercise by the local authority of its mainstream public functions, the local authority lawyer may still act for that charity, but only to the extent that the objects of the charity relate wholly or partly to the local authority area.

Any transactions involving land held on a charitable trust will of course be subject to the constraints set out in Part 7 of the Charities Act 2011, which will, in some circumstances, require statutory advertisement before land can be sold or leased or or an application to the Charity Commission.

Deputyship Orders

A conveyancer working for a social services authority may be asked to act on the sale of a property for a patient who is the subject of a deputyship order made by the Court of Protection in favour of the employing authority or a specified officer of that local authority (identified by job title), such as its Social Services Director.

In that situation, you will be acting not for your employing local authority but instead for the patient the subject of the Deputyship Order. And your instructions will not come from the local authority acting corporately, but from the person named (either personally or by job title) as the Deputy on the Order issued by the Court of Protection. That instruction will usually involve the sale, by auction, of the patient's former home, after they have moved into residential care, with the balance of sale proceeds being paid into a designated account to the credit of that beneficiary.

When acting for such a Deputy, care needs to be taken to ensure that the name on the Deputyship Order (which will not have been drafted by a conveyancer), sufficiently matches the name of the registered proprietor (where the property is registered), or in any other case, that the name of the current owner corresponds to that specified in the latest conveyance or transfer.

Any minor discrepancies between the beneficiary's name as stated on the Order authorising the sale and the name as written on the title would need to be covered off in the Special Conditions of Sale, to avoid complications arising when the transaction is about to complete. Remember also, that a Deputyship Order can only subsist whilst the named beneficiary of that order remains alive.

If that beneficiary (being already elderly and frail), dies before completion of the transaction, the Order will immediately lapse and their property will become part of their estate, to be dealt with according to their will or intestacy.

Therefore, it is important, on a deputyship sale, that you include a provision entitling the named deputy to rescind the contract (without penalty save as regards the return of any deposit previously paid), if the person who is the subject of the deputyship order either dies before completion the transaction or if there is some other frustrating event relating to the deputyship order which prevents a timely completion of the sale.

Financial matters

A challenge for many local authority conveyancers is how to exchange and complete on a transaction without access to a solicitor's client account. It is that SRA regulated account which is at the core of mainstream conveyancing in the UK. It keeps clients' money separate from the solicitor's own money, which means that even if that solicitor gets into financial difficulty, a client's money will always be safe.

Provided that the correct protocols are followed, a transfer of funds between the client accounts of two solicitors or licensed conveyancers is also the most effective way to protect monetary transfers against fraud or mistake. It is why the Standard Conditions of Sale and the Standard Commercial Property Conditions, which, between them, govern almost all conveyancing transactions in England and Wales, insist that transfers of deposits and completion money are made between solicitors' clients' accounts and never directly between clients directly.

But it is the ability of solicitors and licensed conveyancers to give professional undertakings to each other regarding the transmission and receipt of funds which oils the wheels of the conveyancing process. At the point contracts are exchanged, a buyer's lawyer will give the seller's lawyer, a professional undertaking to transfer the contract deposit to the seller's solicitor's client account.

The seller's solicitor will, in turn, unless the contract states otherwise, undertake to hold the transfer deposit in its client account pending completion of the transaction, when it will be amalgamated with the balance of the purchase money.

When the contractual completion date comes round, the buyer's solicitor will transfer the balance of the purchase money to the seller's solicitor's client account, usually against a professional undertaking from the seller's solicitor, to hold the balance of the purchase money to order until completion itself has been formalised by a telephone call.

Before completion takes place, the seller's solicitor will have also undertaken to transfer funds to clear off any existing mortgage on the seller's title and procure evidence of that discharge.

If the seller's conveyancer has undertaken to comply with the Law Society's Code for Completion by Post 2019, that will provide an additional warranty from the seller's conveyancer, that they are able to provide a good receipt for the purchase money and that they have carried out the required due diligence checks to ensure that their client is the rightful owner of the property being sold and therefore entitled to receive the purchase money. But how do you act for the vendor or purchaser in a conveyancing transaction when you do not have access to a regulated client account, particularly if the transfer of your client's funds to another party or the management of monies received by your client in relation to a sale is not within your direct control? Several consequences flow from this:

* You cannot undertake to transfer funds to another party.

* You cannot hold money on account (including mortgage funds).

* You cannot undertake to hold money to order.

* You cannot hold money as stakeholder.

* You cannot undertake to discharge a mortgage or clear off other financial liabilities.

* You cannot process any conveyancing transaction involving the transfer of money in a way which is compliant with the Standard Conditions of Sale or Standard Commercial Property Conditions.

If there was no flexibility over any of these issues, an in-house conveyancer without access to a regulated client-account, would not be able to exchange contracts on or complete any property transaction involving an exchange of money. If that was the end of it, the bulk of local authority convincing work would have to be outsourced to external firms of solicitors because those in-house conveyancing teams would be no facility to deal with the matter in house.

What makes the system work is the willingness of lawyers acting for both parties to work around the rules in a way which neither infringes anti money laundering regulations nor puts money belonging to any client at risk. We will look at this in more detail in a later chapter. In the meantime, we go back to the professional rules themselves.

The SRA Standards and Regulations 2019 which replaced the SRA handbook 2011, allows solicitors to deliver non-reserved legal services to the public on behalf of a business that is not authorised by a legal services regulator. It is this change, which expressly allows local authorities with in-house solicitors to use their in-house capability to provide legal advice to other local authorities, such as by extending it services beyond its own organization.

In its 13th July, 2021 Law Society Practice Note, *"Solicitors Offering Legal Services to the Public from Unregulated Entities"*, local authority lawyers employed in-house and using their in-house capability to provide legal advice to other local authorities, and thereby extending services beyond their own organisation, is interpreted as providing legal services to a section of the public. The guidance goes on to state that individual solicitors working for unregulated entities (being any organisation which is not registered as a law-firm with the SRA) must comply with the SRA Code of Conduct for Solicitors, even though the organisation for which they work will not be bound by the SRA Code of Conduct for Firms. It emphasises that all solicitors are subject to the SRA **principles,** as previously outlined.

When it comes to money, the general rule is that an in-house solicitor working for any organisation, other than a regulated firm of solicitors, is not authorised to hold client money. Client money is defined for this purpose to include: money paid by clients on account of legal fees or third-party disbursement costs; any damages that a client receives as part of a settlement of their case; the assets of any estate; any money held on the client's behalf to complete a transaction or for investment purposes. Whilst this does not prevent an in-house solicitor being a signatory to a bank account held by an employer in its own name, it must be made clear to clients that it is the employer, and not the solicitor, that is holding the money.

Another permissible option, is the placing of client funds into an escrow account under the control of a third party.

Third Part Managed Accounts

In Rule 11 of its 2019 revision of the Solicitors Accounts Rules, the SRA has given official recognition to the use of third party managed accounts, as an alternative way of holding client money. In its guidance ,'Third Party Managed Accounts (TPMA's)', updated to November 2019, which is written primarily for regulated firms of solicitors as an alternative to the traditional solicitors' client account, the SRA makes the point that money held in a TPMA does not fall under the definition of client money in the SRA Accounts Rules as it is not held or received by solicitors.

As such, it does not have to be held in accordance with SRA Rules relating to the holding of client money. However, Rule 11 of the Solicitors Accounts Rules will still apply to anyone using a TPMA and appropriate steps must be taken to comply with the requirements set out.

The SRA defines a Third Party Managed Account as *"any account held at a bank or building society to the name of a third party which is an authorised payment institution or small payment institution that has chosen to implement the safeguarding arrangements in accordance with the Payment Services Regulations (as defined in the Payment Services Regulations 2017) regulated by the Financial Conduct Authority, in which monies are owned beneficially by the third party and which is operated upon terms agreed between the third party and your client as an escrow payment service."*

To comply with the Rule 11.1 and 11.2 of the Solicitors Accounts Rules, anyone using a TPMA provider must:

- Take reasonable steps, as set out below, to make sure that the client is informed of and understand their rights and obligations and what the use of the TPMA means in their case, including whether they are required to authorise payments, and any charges or fees they are liable to pay;

- Obtain regular statements and ensure that these reflect the transactions on the account correctly, and make sure that the funds in the TPMA are only used for the designated purpose;
- Maintain an overview of the transactions on the account and keep appropriate records to reflect this.

Where a TPMA is to be used, reasonable steps must be taken to ensure that a client understands the arrangement before it is entered into. Clients should understand in particular: how the money will be held and how the transaction will work; the right to terminate the agreement; that the TPMA is regulated by the Financial Conduct Authority; and that complaints about the TPMA provider should be made to that provider in accordance with their complaints procedure; and that the regulatory protections that applied to TPMAs are different to those that apply to client money held in a solicitor's client account.

Furthermore, suitable arrangements must be in place for the use and monitoring TPMAs in accordance with SRA regulatory arrangements, including having internal systems for monitoring transactions on the account and keeping appropriate records.

Third party managed accounts are still very much a new market for solicitors and there is, as yet, no noticeable use of TPMAs by local authorities. Shieldpay are amongst a small number of providers of offering TPMA's in this restricted market.

Anyone proposing to use a third party managed account in the ordinary course of a conveyancing transaction would need to ensure that the contract enables the solicitor acting for the local authority to send and receive funds in this way. Such contractual issues are addressed in more detail in a later chapter.

Of course, there is little point in an in-house conveyancer having use of a TPMA to hold client monies, including stakeholder monies and to pay and receive transactional funds, unless that conveyancing team also has direct control over money is coming in and out of that account.

Piecework Vs Hourly Rates

Another difference between external solicitors' firms and an in-house conveyancing team is the way they are paid. For private law firms, the general rule for transactional work is that the solicitor's firm is paid on completion of a transaction and will be held to its original quote for the work, unless during the course of the transaction complications had arisen which the conveyancer could not realistically have previously foreseen.

In fact, the SRA Transparency Rules, which were introduced in 2019, now make is a legal requirement that regulated solicitors firms which undertake conveyancing work, must publish, amongst other things, adequate details of its fees for a typical transaction, including: the total cost of the service or, where this is not practicable, the average cost or range of costs; the basis for charges, including any hourly rates or fixed fees.

Such fee information must be clear and accessible and in a prominent place on a solicitor's website. Whilst there is nothing obvious in the transparency rules requiring private conveyancers to offer a fixed-price conveyancing, it is such pricing information which most prospective clients would expect to receive when shopping around for a conveyancing service.

By contrast, most in-house lawyers, including agency and locum staff, are appointed on a fixed salary or hourly-rate, which is not dependent on the number of transactions on which they exchange or complete. Client departments, are also be charged for those same legal services, on the same hourly basis. It means that the financial imperative to exchange and complete transactions in volume does not exist in local government in quite the same way as it does in private practice.

Often, the only time in which the internal cost of a local authority transaction becomes relevant, is when a third party being asked to bear the council's legal costs in relation to that transaction. The third party will not be invoiced directly by the council's legal department as legal services are not been provided directly to that third party. Instead, what is being sought in those circumstances, is an agreed contribution by that third party towards the council's internal legal and administrative costs. And as local authority legal departments cannot charge VAT to its own host-organisation, it follows that there is no VAT cost to be reimbursed by the third party.

Professional Indemnity Insurance

The SRA does not require an in-house solicitor performing work for their own employer to obtain mandatory professional Indemnity Insurance in accordance with its minimum terms and conditions.

Law Society Practice Note *"In-house practice: Regulatory Requirements"*, published September 2022, explains that the liability of in-house solicitors should normally be covered by their employment contract and principles of vicarious liability. As such, while it is for an employer to decide whether or not it is necessary to obtain insurance, each in-house solicitor should consider their own position carefully and potential exposure to claims.

The position is even more complex when an in-house solicitor is not only acting for their own employer but for other third-party organisations for whom they are authorized to provide legal services. Remember also that the primary purpose of professional Indemnity Insurance is not to protect solicitors but to protect clients in the event that they suffer loss as a result of the legal mal-practice.

The same is true as regards the laws governing an employer's vicarious liability. It protects the third party who has suffered loss not the solicitor-employee who caused that loss. Agency-lawyers who are not employed directly by the local authority will usually, as part of their engagement, be required to produce evidence of their professional insurance, arranged through the agency through whom they work. If, through their local authority employment, an in-house solicitor is asked to act for a client who is not their employer, SRA rules require that the client is informed that the lawyer is not required to have professional Indemnity Insurance that meets the SRA minimum terms and conditions and explain what alternative insurance arrangements are in place and, if requested, provide information about what this covers.

Law Society guidance also recommends that it is made clear to these clients the differences between the insurance cover which is being offered and the SRA's minimum terms and conditions, which would apply if they are instructed an external firm of solicitors. Such clients must also be informed that they will not be eligible for a grant from the SRA Compensation Fund, accompanied by an explanation that the Compensation Fund is a discretionary fund operated by the SRA to which all solicitors contribute, its purpose being to make grants to people whose money has been stolen, mis-appropriated or otherwise not properly accounted for; or for those who have suffered a loss for which a regulated person should have been insured, but was not.

Engagement with Clients

In this section we are talking about those clients, other than the solicitor's own employer, for whom the professional rules allow an in-house solicitor to act.

To meet regulatory obligations, these clients need to be provided with sufficient detailed information to enable them to make an informed choice about the service they are purchasing. Law society guidance recommends that such information is provided in a way that it is readable to clients; using simple plain language and avoiding jargon where possible; provides clear explanations where appropriate, together with details of the consumer protections that apply; and which make sure that the required information is accessible and that clients will not easily miss it.

The Code of Conduct also requires solicitors to establish and maintain, or participate in, an adequate complaints handling procedure. In particular, at the time of engagement, clients must be informed about: the right to complain about the service is provided and charges made for that service; how a complaint can be made and to whom; any complaint can be made, and when they can take their complaint to the legal ombudsman and when they can make any such complaint.

If a complaint is made and not resolved to the client satisfaction within eight weeks, a solicitor is required to provide the following information in writing, namely: the client's right to complain to the legal ombudsman including relevant time frames and contact information; if the internal complaints procedure has been exhausted and the complaint cannot be settled, to identify an alternative dispute resolution approved body that could deal with the complaint and state whether the solicitor or agrees to use the scheme operated by that body.

Every professional organisation should have a formal complaint handling process, which should cover: acknowledging the complaint if it cannot be addressed immediately and giving the client details of the process, including the fact that it is free of charge, with likely timescales and contact information- ideally within two working days; how the complaint will be investigated; and determining the outcome of the investigation.

If no poor service has been found, a full explanation should be provided to the client as to how this conclusion has been arrived at. If poor service has been found, to identify appropriate remedies.

Where Professional Indemnity Insurance is in place, consideration should be given as to when it is appropriate to notify any insurer about the complaint and proposals for its remedy. But note that an admission of liability to a client may have implications for professional Indemnity Insurance. The Law Society guidance also recommendeds use of the following texts for use in correspondence with clients once a complaints process has been exhausted:

"We have been unable to settle your complaint using our internal complaints process. You have a right to complain to the legal ombudsman, an independent complaints body, established under the Legal Services Act 2007, that deals with legal services complaints. You have six months from the date of this, our final letter, in which to complain to the legal ombudsman
Legal ombudsman

PO box 6806

Wolverhampton

WV1 9WJ

Telephone: 0300 555 0333

E-mail address: enquiries@legalombudsman.org.uk;

Website: www.legalombudsman.org.uk"

Conflicts of Interest

SRA Principles require solicitors to act with independence, honesty, integrity and in the best interests of their client. But in-house conveyancers may face particular ethical challenges in situations where an employer's commercial or political objectives compete with those professional obligations.

In-house solicitors should therefore set clear expectations with their line-management concerning their own professional obligations, in particular, the fact that these obligations cannot be overridden and must be maintained or even when there is tension from other business or political demands.

This is also important for the public reputation of the business. Law society guidance also recommends that, where it is possible to do so, a clause could be inserted into an employment contract outlining that solicitors are under an overriding obligation to comply with their duties as a solicitor and that the employer must not therefore put the solicitor in conflict with this. Alternatively, this could be set out in an internal memorandum with an employer or line manager.

SRA rules prohibit a solicitor from acting in a matter, or a particular aspect of the matter, if they have a conflict of interest or there is a significant risk of such a conflict, Rule 6.2 of the solicitors code of conduct permits a solicitor to act for more than one client and the same matter in circumstances where either:

a) The clients have a substantially common interest in relation to the matter or the aspect of it, as appropriate, or
b) The clients are competing for the same objective and that the conditions below are met, namely: (i) all the clients have given informed consent, given or evidenced to you in writing, to you acting; (ii) where appropriate, you put in place effective

safeguards to protect your clients' confidential information; (iii) you are satisfied it is reasonable for you to act for all of the clients.

Note also Rule 8.1 of the Solicitors Code of Conduct which applies in all cases and which states: *"You identify who you are acting for in relation to any matter."*

It is clear from the above that there may be many circumstances where an in-house lawyer can safely act for more than one party in relation to the same matter.

This is most likely to arise in circumstances where the in-house legal department is asked to act simultaneously for the local authority employer as well as for a subsidiary organisation, such as a council-controlled company (see above).

It might also arise where the legal department is acting for a joint committee on which several councils are represented. Or in a transaction where the same legal team are asked to act for two local authorities in a joint purchase or sale of a property.

Even in circumstances where the same legal team can act for more than one client in a single transaction, it is important that each is treated as a separate client in terms of client-care correspondence and follow up advice. Where it is practical to do so, a further safeguard may be to appoint a separate fee earner within each team. This should not involve any significant duplication of work but means that each client has a separate fee earner dedicated to their interest.

It is also to avoid the possibility of conflicts of interest arising that a conflict - check should be carried out whenever a new file is opened. Often, when a property address is typed into your case management system, you will discover other files (both open and closed) which deal other aspects relating to the same property. Carrying out this electronic conflict-check and also to avoid accidental duplication of work previously carried out by another fee earner in respect of the same property.

Client Confidentiality

Running alongside the rule against conflicts of interest is Rule 6.3 of the SRA Code of Conduct, which places an obligation on every solicitor to keep the affairs of current and former clients confidential unless disclosure is permitted or the client consents.

Particular care must be taken when acting for more than one client in a single transaction, to ensure that the information held by each client remains confidential to that client unless there is mutual agreement to the contrary and such agreement has been recorded in writing. Bolted on to this are the laws relating to Data Protection.

Whilst every local authority will have its own data protection policies, accompanied by the appropriate staff training, no amount of training or due diligence is going to prevent the occasional rogue e-mail going astray and reaching the inbox of the wrong person. That is the nature of emails. You may not have noticed the fact that the address-bar has self-populated with the e-mail address of the wrong person, usually because the unintended recipient has an e-mail address very similar to your intended recipient. Or because you are dealing with two very similar matters at the same time and mistakenly address your e-mail to the wrong solicitor. It just happens.

You may promise yourself that you will never allow it to happen again. It always does. It is then about damage limitation. Let's hope that your rogue e-mail does not contain commercially sensitive information relating to your client or another party, or worse still, personal information about a living individual, which has to be reported as a data-breach, with all the consequences which flow from a data-breach both for yourself as well as the organisation which has vicarious liability for your mistake.

There are various ways to minimize the risk of sensitive information accidentally going astray. The most effective way may be to password protect your sensitive e-mail so that it can only be opened by its intended recipient. That's assuming of course that you have not also sent a password to the wrong person.

A simpler way is to get in the habit of not forwarding e-mail chains on to third parties but instead composing each new e-mail afresh. Clients and other parties may not like it, because everything is no longer in one place. But it gives you 100% control over the content of your message.

If you discover quickly enough that your e-mail has gone to the wrong person, try to use the 'recall' function. Whilst, in most cases, the rogue e-mail will have already reached the recipient's mailbox, the fact that you have to attempted to recall it alerts the recipient of the fact that the e-mail was sent in error.

Where the recipient of the rogue e-mail is another solicitor, they will be under a professional obligation not to misuse information sent to them in error, even if the matter is potentially litigious

In most cases, a simple follow up e-mail to the unintended recipient asking them to delete the rogue e-mail may suffice to close the issue. However, the same protections will not apply if the e-mail is accidentally addressed to someone other than another lawyer or someone having a similar professional responsibility.

Particular care must be taken, when responding to statutory Freedom of Information requests, not to unknowingly release information which is either commercially sensitive or relates to personal data relating to living people which is governed by data protection legislation.

Exemptions preventing the disclosure of both types of information are contained within the Freedom of Information Act 2000, but only so far as it is in the public interest to withhold such information. Withholding such information will always be in the public interest where a commercial transaction is in the process of negotiation or where disclosure could undermine any future negotiations on this or future transactions, where this might undermine third party confidence in the ability of a local authority to keep confidential information secret. When in doubt whether it is legally necessary for sensitive information to be disclosed under FOI, the safer answer will always be 'No'.

So far we have only spoken about transactions under negotiation in relation to FOI. But what about transactions which have already been completed? Many property transactions already fall into the public domain when registered at HM Land Registry, for which open-access is the default position.

It means that anyone can download information about the registered ownership of any property in England and Wales as well as copies of many conveyancing documents, including transfers and leases. The terms of certain statutory agreements, like planning agreements made under Section 106 of the Town and Country Planning Act 1990; or highways agreements made pursuant to sections 38 or 278 of the Highways Act 1980, are kept confidential between the parties up until the date those agreements are completed, when they fall into the public domain and are, in many cases, downloadable from a council website.

Performance Monitoring

One consequence of the compulsory competitive tendering of the 1980s and 1990s was a permanent change in the way local authority legal departments work.

Up until the late 1980s, a local authority legal department was simply part of the wider corporate establishment.

Provided that there was no serious complaint regarding the overall quality and timeliness of the service provided, the lawyers were left to get on with their work. Whilst there was a legal services budget, which might from time to time be the subject of a council-wide financial review, there was no micro-management of the cost of individual fee-earner time. However private practice lawyers had been charging out the cost of their time on individual matters for at least a decade before.

What changed for local authority legal departments at the beginning of the 1990s was a move towards private sector ways of working, at least as regards fee-earner time charging.

Even the term 'fee-earner' is a misnomer for in-house conveyancers, as there are no actual fees to be invoiced. How could there be? How can any organisation invoice itself?

Instead, time-charging within a local authority legal department has enabled managers to monitor the performance of individual conveyancers. But more than that, the introduction of time-charging also enabled local authority legal departments to benchmark the cost of their services against the wider legal market.

Under compulsory competitive tendering (CCT), the collective ability of an in-house legal department to demonstrate that it could deliver a legal service at least as good as anything the local authority could outsource elsewhere, became crucial to its existence. Even where there was no existential threat to an in-house legal department, the overall financial performance of the in-house department may still have a knock-on effect as to what types of work should be outsourced or retained in-house and what changes to the legal service establishments might follow in consequence.

Although compulsory competitive tendering has been gone for more than two decades, many of the hasty internal changes made to respond to it, remained in place as they are just at relevant to the softer Best Value regime which replaced it.

What we have now is a mixed-economy, in which local authority legal work is retained in-house only to the extent that it is cost effective to do so.

Section 3 of the Local Government Act 1999 imposes a Best Value Duty on all but the smallest local authorities, to make arrangements to secure a continuous improvement in the way in which its functions are exercised, having regard to a combination of economy, efficiency and effectiveness. And although the 1999 Act does not impose any duty on local authorities to put their professional services out to tender, as was required under CCT, there is instead a process to be followed, which includes consultation with stakeholders.

The statutory best-value requirement is also supplemented by official government guidance, which is updated from time to time. The economic value provided by an in-house legal department is most likely to come under scrutiny when the finances of the local authority itself are in trouble. A feature of the past two years, leading up to publication of this book, has been the number of local authorities publishing statutory notices under section 114 of the Local Government Finance Act 1988.

Given that a local authority cannot actually go bankrupt in the true sense of the word, the issue of a Section 114 Notice is the nearest thing to bankruptcy and alerts the world that the local authority issuing a notice cannot pay its way from the income it receives.

In its September 2022 Report, *'Learning Lessons: what Section 114 can teach us'* The Chartered Institute of Public Finance and Accountancy (CIPFA), reviewed evidence from three authorities that have issued section 114 notices in recent years to identify and highlight recurring themes, those local authorities being: Northamptonshire (2018); Croydon (2020); and Slough (2021).

Each of those local authorities were very different entities, comprising a county council; a London borough; and the third smallest unitary council. Since publication of the CIPFA report, Birmingham City Council has added itself to the list.

In its Executive Summary, CIPFA summarises common symptoms as being: over-ambitious savings (particularly where historic records show that savings have not been achieved); lack of a medium-term financial plan (which should indicate an understanding and assurance that supports financial sustainability); leadership issues (particularly where there has been changes at senior level); inadequate governance (where audits and governance committees have not exercised their functions nor understood their roles); weak financial management (whose reporting and monitoring should provide assurance and evidence for effective budgetary decision-making); and lack of reserves (with organisations that have little or no reserves facing significantly higher risks).

In its page five introduction, CIPFA explains the purpose of Section 114, *"which sets out the duty of the chief finance officer to make a section 114 report if it appears that the expenditure of the authority incurred (including expenses it proposes to incur) in any financial year is likely to exceed the resources (including sums borrowed) available to it to meet that expenditure"*. Issuing the section 114 notice immediately suspends all financial activity apart from that which is necessary to maintain statutory duties.

It also initiates a 21-day period for Full Council to consider the report and agree urgent action to start to remedy the situation. The authority's external auditors and the appropriate government department will also be notified and can step in to provide advice and support.

The issue of insolvent local authorities is further explored in researcher Mark Sandford's 13th September, 2023 Insight Report to the

UK Parliament titled, *What happens if a council goes bankrupt?*' In which he states, *"A Section 114 Notice means the council cannot make new spending commitments and must meet within 21 days to discuss what to do next. Previously, most councils in this situation then passed an amended budget reducing spending on services, which is what happened after the severe financial problems in Northamptonshire (2018) and Croydon (2020. At the start of the 2020s, a number of councils facing financial difficulties sought capitalisation direction from the government, providing special permission to use their capital funds, for instance, from selling assets or property-to top- up service spending.*

Capitalisation directions have sometimes been incorrectly described as bailouts. Although the government has powers to intervene in how councils' services are run, this does not happen automatically when a section 114 notices issued. However, many councils that have issued section 114 notices have subsequently been subject to intervention: these have included Woking Borough Council, Slough Borough Council, Thurrock Council, Nottingham City Council and the London borough of Croydon".

Marginally less serious than the issue of a statutory Section 114 notice, are the Best Value notices issued by central government, most recently to Eastleigh Borough Council as well as to Runnymede Borough Council.

A Best Value notice is a formal notification that the Government has concerns regarding an authority and includes a request that the local authority engages with the government department to provide assurance of improvement. The Government then expects authorities that have been issued with best value notices to continue leading their own improvement.

In the case of a 19 December, 2023 Best Value Notice issued to Eastleigh Borough Council, the Minister was concerned was that the authority has significant debt relative to its size, being 45 times its core spending power, which had been used to acquire a commercial regeneration and housing investment portfolio; secondly, shortages in terms of capacity and expertise in the authority's asset management team, as well as its finance and internal audit, which has impacted its capacity to manage the scale and ambition of its commercial and housing developments.

In the case of the Best Value Notice issued to Runnymede Borough Council, on 19 December, 2023, the Minister's concerns were that the authority had a significant debt relative to its size amounting to borrowing of 71 times its core spending power, used predominantly to invest in the authority's property portfolio. Again, this level of debt poses the authority with capacity challenges, particularly in asset management, commercial and regeneration activity. A second concern was that commercial income represented a substantial revenue source for Runnymede Borough Council and used to support both core and discretionary services, which exposed the authority to significant financial risks should anticipated income fall.

Although the provision of legal services (either in-house or external) has so far received no specific mention in relation to a section 114 Notice or a Best Value Notice, it is easy to see how the work of any in-house legal team would be impacted if the local authority is forced to scale back its transactional work.

This might include an immediate halt to any prospective purchases where contracts have yet to exchange. Whilst at the same time, there could be pressure to speed up the state of assets not immediately required for the council's functional work. Though there is no guarantee that progressing of those sales would go to the existing in-house legal service, which might be a decision for the commissioners appointed to oversee the council's insolvency. Maybe a decision for any commissioners appointed to oversee the councils insolvency. At that point, the efficiency of the council's in-house legal service may come under the same scrutiny as other head - office functions.

Anti Money-Laundering

For private firms of solicitors, anti-money-laundering due diligence is primarily about 'know your client' and knowing the source of funds. But you already know your client. It is the organization that employs you. Although as has already been seen, professional rules do not restrict a solicitor employed by a local authority to acting only for that authority. The Local Authorities (Goods and Services)Act 1970 and its associated regulations, lists hundreds of organisations to whom you could theoretically provide legal services within the terms of your existing employment.

Most, if not all, of that extensive list of organisations would be designated as 'low risk' under Regulation 37 of the Money Laundering, Terrorist Financing and Transfer of Funds (Information on the Payer) Regulations 2017, because they are concerned with public administration or are publicly owned organisations. And if you are dealing with another firm of solicitors, you are entitled to place reliance on the fact that the firm with whom you are dealing, should already have carried out the required due diligence in relation to their own client and the transaction, before even acknowledging instructions.

For the same reason, it is important that when transmitting completion monies to another firm of solicitors, you ensure that they have first undertaken to comply with the Law Society's Code for Completion by Post 2019.

Compliance with the 2019 code means that the law firm receiving completion monies, warrants that the person to whom the money is being paid is entitled to receive it and that the solicitor's firm can provide a good receipt for that money.

In other words, it provides an additional safeguard for the buyer's lawyer who is transmitting the completion monies. But that doesn't mean that in-house local authority lawyers are exempt from the need to comply with the Proceeds of Crime Act 2002 or the 2017 Regulations. Because anti-money laundering doesn't only apply to 'know your client' due diligence.

The full extent of anti-money-laundering responsibilities and the criminal sanctions for any breach, are set out in the Proceeds of Crime Act 2002 and its associated regulations. These include the general obligation to report a suspicious transaction and not to do anything which could amount to 'tipping off' a suspect.

There are many factors which can make a transaction suspicious, even when there is another firm of solicitors acting on the other end of your transaction.

Every legal practice, including an in-house team of lawyers, should have its own documented policy for dealing with anti-money-laundering due diligenceand provide training to its staff. It's about knowing what makes a transaction suspicious? Who to report those suspicions to? And how to protect your local authority client from fraud. And remember not to take everything at face value. It is possible to impersonate another firm of solicitors, in the same way as it is possible to impersonate any individual, including the registered owner of a property.

It's why, whenever monies are transferred between accounts, there are now conveyancing protocols in place designed to reduce the risk of fraud, including the risk of monies innocently going astray because of an accounting or transmission error.

Like mis-typing an e-mail address, it is the easiest thing in the world to mis- type the number of a bank account, perhaps by transposing figures. That mistake only comes to light when the money doesn't arrive at its intended destination. It's why it is always better to have bank details provided on headed notepaper. And why it's important for the person transmitting the money to speak on the telephone to someone in the receiving organisation, just to make sure that the bank details are absolutely correct.

A higher level of due diligence is required on the part of the local authority conveyancer, when the other party has not engaged a professional conveyancer to act for them in the transaction, perhaps because of its limited value. None of the conveyancing conventions designed to protect against fraud or mistake when transmitting funds will then apply.

See the next section in this chapter, which deals with situations where you are transacting with someone who has not engaged a professional conveyancer.

A key difference between an in-house legal department working for local authority and an external firm of solicitors, is that the in-house team would not usually have direct control over the transfer of funds and the management of the incoming capital receipts. Someone else is usually paid to do that.

Usually that person will be a senior accountant within the local authority's finance team. Their duties will also include the need to undertake the necessary due diligence AML checks to avoid the council falling victim to fraud or the innocent mistakes which can lead to deposits and completion money going astray, and perhaps lost for ever.

So short of standing behind that accountant and looking over their shoulder whilst they make that crucial funds-transfer, how far is it your responsibility to make sure that those funds reach their intended recipient?

It is of course your responsibility to make sure that the senior accountant actioning the funds-transfer has the correct information in front of them to safely action that funds-transfer. This means that it is primarily down to you, or at least in the first instance, to verify source of funds (where money is incoming) and that you have undertaken the required due diligence to ensure that the account details which you provide to your local authority accountant are absolutely correct.

This will include obtaining from the other solicitor involved in the transaction, details of a contact at that firm, who can be telephoned buy your council's finance team,to confirm bank details. These precautionary measures on your part do not absolve the local authority accounts team from the need for them to carry out their own due diligence checks relating to the transaction and the recipient bank details, before actioning the payment. It just reduces the risk of fraud or monies innocently going astray.

The SRA regularly puts out updated guidance to firms on anti-money-laundering, usually as a result of 'lessons learned'. Amongst such advice is a template client/matter risk report, which is designed to be adapted and used whenever a firm takes on a new client or starts a new matter, even for an existing client. Please take a few minutes to look at it.

Writing in the Law Society's Gazette, 19 February, 2024, Weightmans Partner, Susanna Heley, provides practical tips on how to avoid 'Friday afternoon fraud', where the fraudster hacks in to a solicitor's client account and then provides false bank details to clients of that firm who are about to transmit funds to exchange contracts or complete their purchase. It is called Friday afternoon fraud, because that is the date most residential conveyancing transactions complete, giving clients the weekend to unpack and complete their house-move. It is why Friday is always the most stressful day of the week for most conveyancing solicitors, as they juggle multiple back-to-back completions, making sure that monies are received and transmitted on time and that they have everything else they need in front of them to complete those transactions. Get it wrong and a client's house-move may have to be aborted at the last minute, even if a moving-van is already on route.

So Friday is the day when everyone is tense and chasing around, which makes it the ideal day of the week for conveyancing fraudsters.

Heley's advice was prompted by an SRA decision fining a solicitor £26,000 (including costs), when that solicitor negligently paid away monies to a fraudulent account, supposedly on the client's instructions, when in fact the email traffic between that solicitor and their clients had been intercepted by the fraudster.

The day before the transaction was due to complete, that solicitor had received an e-mail from a slightly differently email account but purportedly from the client, requesting that the proceeds of sale be paid to an account or other than that which the client had previously provided. The solicitor properly got back to the client saying they would need telephone confirmation of the changed instructions. However, that telephone conversation never took place.

Instead the solicitor received a further e-mail confirming the changed account details, against which the solicitor or agreed to send funds the following Monday. The mistake was only discovered when the bank notified the solicitor, nearly two weeks later that it had concerns about the recipient account.

Although the loss was made good by the firm's insurers and no formal complaint was forthcoming from the client, the matter still reached the SRA, which noted that despite the bank raising suspicions, the solicitor only reported the loss to the firm's insurers.

Amongst other findings, the SRA said that, for an experienced conveyancer, the last-minute change in instructions was a red flag the solicitor shouldn't have missed. It was also neither necessary nor prudent to send funds to the new account the next business day. The solicitor should have known that the circumstances were suspicious and worthy of proper investigation to prevent fraud.

The failure to insist on additional verification measures was particularly troubling given the critical importance of such steps to counter fraud and attempted criminality.

Although there was no question of dishonesty or lack of integrity on the solicitor's part, SRA guidance makes clear that there is an expectation that solicitor's report such cases, even where fraudulently obtained or stolen money has been replaced.

In her commentary on the decision, Heley states that all solicitors should be alert to Friday afternoon fraud, which are targeted attacks on homebuyers and conveyancers when property transactions are completed. And that email modification fraud is the most common type of cyber attack reported to the SRA, amounting to 68% of reports in 2020. *Heley offers the following five suggestions to reduce the risk of Friday afternoon fraud:*

1. *Train staff to spot signs of a potentially fraudulent or e-mail. Was the e-mail expected or does it change previous instructions regarding the provision of bank details? Is the e-mail address correct, including the domain name and are there any hidden details in the e-mail, such as embedded links, unknown or similar e-mail addresses?*
2. *Raise client awareness about your processes and procedures. Warn those clients that you would never change bank details by e-mail and educate those clients about the risks of cyber fraud. Also ensure that staff feel confident about querying and checking payment transfer requests, even under pressure.*
3. *Identify the contact. Pick up the phone but avoid calling numbers containing red flags. Take the time to be certain of client details as time pressure is often a factor in making mistakes. Get bank details at a face-to-face meeting or verify them by phone early on. Be clear that e-mail changes will not be accepted without direct confirmation from a named contact.*
4. *Know your reporting requirements. If a suspicious transaction has gone through, reporting obligations must be considered immediately. You will*

need to inform: your bank; the National Fraud and Cyber Crime Reporting Centre on 0300123 2040; your professional indemnity insurer (or line manager and practice management for an in-house service); the SRA on 0121 329-6827 or e-mail fraud@sra.org.uk.

5. *Get advice from the Law Society. Such advice can include cyber security guidance; information on the availability of cyber insurance; and free and confidential support from a fellow solicitor through the Practice Advice Service.*

Perhaps it is entirely fortuitous that, at the time of writing, there are no publicised cases of public money going astray as a result of conveyancing fraud. But it could be a disaster waiting to happen. Don't be the first one to get caught out. **If in doubt, report!**

4 IN-HOUSE SURVIVAL

In the last chapter we mentioned the move towards time - charging for services provided by an in-house legal department for its corporate client. But even in private practice, time charging does not necessarily translate directly into invoices issued against a client, particularly for transactional work where both the clients and the conveyancer that are working towards a fixed legal budget, as required by the Transparency Rules.

What time challenging does instead is to measure the actual cost of the transaction tor the organisation delivering the legal service. Nor is time-charging an accurate measure of individual fee - earner performance. Time charging does no more than measure the actual time spent by an individual fee-earner on a piece of work. It doesn't measure how efficiently that piece of work was carried out by the fee earner. In fact, time charging could be said to be a system which rewards inefficiency, as it will always be the slowest and most inefficient lawyer who charges out the most time for the particular piece of work.

What is more important for any organisation is what a fee-earner achieves in terms of productivity for each hour they have worked. In other words, it is not just about time-spent but more about unit - cost. How efficiently any fee earner can work, depends not only on the skills and motivation of that fee earner but also on the efficiency of the environment within which they work.

How to work efficiently

Efficiency is about making the best use of resources, both at an individual as well as at a team - level. It is about reducing unit-cost.

In terms of time-charging, the faster you can complete a transaction without compromising on accuracy or the quality of the service you provide, the cheaper the cost of that transaction both your team and your client.

More likely than not, those resources will not include any secretarial support in the traditional sense of the word. Instead, most local authority fee earners are now expected to produce their own correspondence and documentation using the case management system provided. But there are practical ways in which individual fee-earners, as well as the teams in which they work, can increase the efficiency of their output, particularly when a fee earner has no resource other than the computer screen which is in front of them. Here are some suggestions:

- Never type a document. Always dictate-dictate-dictate. Because even if you can touch type, you can't type as fast as you can speak. Any computer which is Windows 10 or higher will have a voice- dictation facility built in. Though you may have to find it on your computer and enable it. And using voice-recognition software is not the same having a competent secretary who can transcribe your work. It cannot interpret what you are trying to say. It will type exactly what it thinks you have said. For example, if I dictate the word 'comma', it will tell me to, "call my mum". If I dictate the word 'draft', as in document, I will get the draught which comes in through the window behind me. If I dictate the word 'sealing', as in the attestation of a corporate document, I will get the ceiling which is above my head. So why do I use voice dictation? Because even with its faults, it is still three times quicker than if I had to type every word longhand.
- If you have access to an electronic case management system, spend an extra minute labelling up each item as you import it into the case - file, so that you can find it instantly using the

search facility. Also use any electronic subject - file which is provided to store this and similar items. The extra minute per item you have spent doing this, may save you, or another fee - earner, hours, six months down the line, if it means not having to trawl through the entire file to find that elusive document or email.

- Make the best use of Microsoft Teams to attend meetings online instead taking half a day out to travel to a face-to-face meeting. There is a time and place for a face-to-face meeting, perhaps if you're meeting a new client for the first time and want to make a good impression.
- Try to keep non-chargeable time, such as on -line training, outside of the sacred 10:00 a.m. to 4:00 p.m. core hours slot. Those core hours should be reserved for fee - earning.
- Wherever you are working, make sure that you have access to the right equipment to produce work quickly. Unless you have micro fingers, please do not use the miniature keyboard which forms part of your laptop. Instead, wire up a separate finger-friendly- keyboard, which enables you to type quickly. Buy it from Tesco if you need to. Ditto-a wired mouse. Get a wide-screen monitor, so that you can see your work without squinting. And of course a headset, for your team's meetings and also to enable you to dictate your work without disturbing other people around you.
- Get into the habit of using the Land Registry's digital registration at the outset of any transaction involving the purchase of whole titles. This is explained in greater detail in a later chapter.
- If you can, always use live time-recording if available and always keep that timer switched on during those core hours, except when you are taking a break. Remember that no one will ever thank you for undercharging. Not your client, which has already budgeted for your work. Not your colleagues, who will have to work that bit harder to compensate for your under-

performance. Not your line – manager, who takes responsibility for the collective performance of the team.

Getting Into Management – Your Chance to Make a Difference

Here, we are talking about middle management. You are the captain leading your troop, not the general sitting in your oak panelled office far away from battle.

If you work within a large legal department there will always be management opportunities arising from time to time, many of which may not be permanent.

Some of these temporary management opportunities might be planned, such as someone going on maternity leave. Or it could be sudden and unplanned, like the chief executive who fell out of a tree. Yes - it really happened!

Going into management doesn't just look good on a CV. Leadership is valuable life skill. It is your opportunity to make a difference. To put your own ideas into effect. To make the changes, which you always wanted to make but never had the seniority to implement. To create the team you want to create. To re-set those client relationships which had previously become soured.

In practice most local authority management is a combination of administration and leadership. But it is down to you, how much time you spend dealing with the administrative chores and how much effort you put into leadership.

In the context of administration, there are the endless staff-appraisals and half-year appraisals; attendance at management team meetings; and recruitment, both temporary and permanent. Management styles vary in how much time is devoted to administrative tasks compared with leadership. But whatever happens, the time spent dealing with those administrative tasks should not balloon to the exclusion of everything else. And even those administrative tasks can provide opportunities for you to demonstrate good leadership. So what makes a good manager? Here are some suggestions:

- You look, act and sound like a manager. One of the first things which you might notice when you step into management is that it changes the way other people react to you. Not only the staff reporting to you. But other people as well. You are no longer one of the guys. You are the face of authority. It has to be like that, otherwise you would not be able to deal with the difficult things, like managing under-performance. Whether or not your team like you, you have to be able to command their respect.
- You do your best to create an environment in which your staff are able to work efficiently. It is about making sure that they have the best systems within which they do their work and that those systems work as well as they can. Any distractions from productive work must be kept to a minimum. Whilst convening staff meetings are an essential part of management, they must be kept to the business in hand. As you are leading the meeting, it is your job to keep discussion focused on the agenda. To brief the team on the things they need to be briefed and to provide an opportunity for constructive feedback. It should not degenerate into a grumble-session or a social chit-chat, more suited to a coffee-break. And try to keep it to the time you have allocated for it. Because all staff-meetings mean that there is less time for staff to do their chargeable-work. So don't blame them when the monthly figures come in below target. There is no law that says that the meeting scheduled for two hours has to last for two hours if you can get through the core business in 30 minutes. Remember that everyone's time has a value. And remember that every awayday spent out of the office, 'bonding', has a hidden cost above the tea and biscuits and hire of the venue. Can your team really afford to lose a day's revenue? And here are two little secrets. The first is that some staff love awaydays, particularly if there are quizzes and cake-competitions. But most staff only go along because your senior management has told them to. Wouldn't they rather be doing their jobs? The second little secret is that when the biggest multi-nationals organise awaydays for their staff, they

usually do so over the course of a long weekend. But astonishingly, no one ever complains or demands time off in lieu. Why? Would you complain about being given a free all-inclusive weekend at one of the UK's top golfing-hotels – even if you don't like golf?

- The focus of your team is always outwards towards service delivery and clients. Not inwards towards itself. If your team does not deliver for its clients, what is the point of its existence? Let somebody else to the navel gazing.
- You take the trouble to know everything that is going on in your team. Like Lord Alan Sugar, you know every nut and bolt in your team's product. This is not micro-management. It is about being alert to potential problems before they become a crisis. Electronic case-management systems now make it easy for managers to discreetly dip in and out of individual case files, just to make sure that everything is proceeding as it should, and without those difficult face-to-face meetings with your reportees.
- You are clear in your communications with your team, so that they know exactly what they are asked to do and that there is no scope for misunderstandings.
- Your clients have confidence that you will look after their interests. Even the grumpiest client. They know that you are on their side. That they can turn to you if they have any concerns and receive a prompt and constructive response. You are their troubleshooter. In fact, one of the first things a new manager has to do is to try to repair those client-relationships which previously had not been quite as good as they should have been. You know what your client's expectations are. It is for you to make sure that those expectations are being met, so that their work keeps coming through.
- You lead from the front. You know the job well enough to guide individual members of your team who seek practical advice on operational decisions or solutions to problems. You don't bat questions back with glib put-downs like, 'have you

tried looking it up?' Unless you go further by pointing to a suggested source of reference. You take responsibility for your team's performance. You are not like the chief of police who has never seriously walked the streets and goes into hand-wringing mode whenever there is a major operational failure which they could have prevented. That chief of police would rather let subordinate officers 'hang out to dry' than take any personal criticism. It is the management culture which allowed the Rochdale child abuse scandal to happen. In practical terms, leading from the front can mean that you sit with your team instead of in the glass office at the end of the corridor.

- You recognise talent within your team and are able to 'grow' individual members of your team. It is not just about having people with the right experience, it is also about recognizing someone's potential to gain that experience and become a more valuable member of your team. It is about presenting those staff with assignments which will stretch their potential to the limit. One of the advantages of a 'dip-in-dip out' electronic case management system, is that, like a dual control motor vehicle, you can safely delegate such tasks, knowing that it only takes a moment to take back control if there is a hint that something is about to go wrong.

- You are your team's ambassador. You provide the interface between clients and individual members of your team. You are the person clients will come to the moment they have concerns about the way your team is dealing with their work. If you're not able to respond quickly and positively to those client-concerns, they may simply take their work away and outsource elsewhere. Conversely a job well done, can lead to more work coming through from that particular client including, possibly, entirely new streams of work. You are also someone who is able to repair client-relationships which had previously become damaged before you even begun managing the team. So you are someone who takes the time and trouble to talk to your clients and to understand their expectations and future work-requirements as well as explaining to them what legal services are your team is able to offer over and above what it is already providing to that client?

- Standardise! Standardise! Standardise! If the bulk of your team's work is repetitive volume work, take a tip from Henry Ford. Install a conveyor belt. Metaphorically speaking of course. It means breaking down each volume transaction into a series of repetitive tasks spread between a team of fee earners at varying levels. So someone will be responsible for reviewing the instructions, opening up the file, and downloading land registry documentation and other key information, as well as formally acknowledging those instructions. Someone more senior will review the land-title and identify any issues. Someone will prepare the initial documentation, based on the standard template, and issue it. An experienced conveyancer will deal with the exchange of contracts and bring the transaction to completion, including preparation of the completion statement. Someone else will deal with the post completion work, including submission of the land transaction return, where applicable, and registration formalities. Finally, someone will report back formally to the client regarding the transaction, as completed, with any matters which need to be flagged up for the future. And of course, you will allocate a time-slot for each task. Oh! And don't forget 'quality control.'

- You do whatever is necessary to ensure that in terms of cost, speed of turnaround, and in the quality of the work, what your team can deliver matches favourably with anything which the client would receive if they outsourced to their work to an external law firm. In other words, your benchmark should be that of a commercial firm of similar size, expertise and resource.

- It's all about the presentation. How you present yourself as a manager. How your team presents itself. How engrossments and other legal documentation is presented to clients and other parties. Are those documents professionally bound or are they thrown across as pages of A4 stapled in the corner? But it's not just in the presenting of individual pieces of work but in the presentation of your team as a whole. Do you have a team web page? Then make it your team's shop window. Include on your web page anything which will be of interest to clients or prospective clients. Anything which can help draw attention to the good work which your team does. This should include a posting up of articles on matters of topical legal interest, which can help draw traffic to your team-page. Not just from your own clientel. But also from anyone else who is looking for information on that particular subject, which your team is best placed or to provide. It is about building a profile. Private law firms do it. How often do you Google a legal question, to be presented by an article written by a partner or associate in a law firm who has specific legal expertise in that subject? You are piggybacking on their research. Why not let someone else piggyback on yours? It is all about the PR.

Dealing with an unrepresented party

There is an old legal saying, that the person who is their own solicitor has a fool for a client. But when working within a local authority in-house conveyancing team, you may find yourself dealing with many unrepresented parties.

That doesn't mean they are fools. Just that the value of the transaction may, in their own eyes, be too small to justify employing a solicitor. The other factor is that, unlike commercial organisations, local authorities cannot choose with whom they deal. Nor can you insist that the other person with whom you are dealing obtains proper legal advice and representation. All that you can do is **recommend** that they obtain independent legal advice before entering into a binding contractual commitment.

Whether they heed your recommendation, is entirely up to them. What is more important is that you have made that written recommendation and that you cannot be seen as having done anything to influence the actions of that unrepresented party.

For that reason, it is important that your opening correspondence with that underrepresented party includes the following paragraph, or words to like effect:

"Please note that we act only for [name of council] and are not able to provide you with any legal advice as regards the transaction which you are invited to enter into. It is therefore important that you take independent legal advice from a solicitor or licensed conveyancer before entering into any legal commitment relating to your property. If you already have a solicitor or licensed conveyancer acting for you, please pass this letter and its enclosures across to them and ask your solicitor or licensed conveyancer to contact us directly"

As we have already seen in the earlier section on anti-money-laundering, dealing with an unrepresented party raises a higher risk of fraud or money accidentally going astray, Because none of the conveyancing conventions which apply to transactions between solicitors, can apply when you are transacting with an unrepresented party.

Unless you carry out those a due diligence checks yourself, you have nothing to confirm that the other party is whom they say they are. There are no checks regarding their source of funds. You cannot even be 100% sure with whom you are corresponding, if you are corresponding with an anonymous email account.

Evidence of identity is now a standard Land Registry requirement. Without such evidence, you may be unable to register any transaction concerning property owned-or previously owned- by the unrepresented party.

The safest way to prove identity is to insist that the unrepresented party completes and returns Land Registry form ID1 (or ID2 in the case of a company), which means that they will still have to go to a solicitor or licensed conveyancer with their photo-ID and proof of address.

For the unrepresented party, filling out an ID1 or ID2, and getting it officially signed off involves additional inconvenience and the expense.

Production of a passport and a recent utility bill is only evidence of someone's identity and their address. Further due diligence is then required to verify source of funds, perhaps by seeing and taking a copy of a recent bank statement which is held in the name of that unrepresented party.

Seeing and taking a photocopy of a bank statement also reduces the risk of error when the money is paid out by your local authority to the unrepresented party,

The other issue in dealing with an unrepresented party is that you cannot place reliance on their promise to hold money to order; to transfer funds; deliver correctly executed documents; discharge a mortgage; or comply with any other conveyancing obligation on their part. Because their promise does not carry the weight of a professional undertaking given by another solicitor or licensed conveyancer.

For that reason, you cannot safely complete a transaction with an unrepresented third party unless you already have in your possession everything which you need to complete that transaction. It also means that you cannot safely transfer funds to that third party until after the transaction has been completed and everything has been dated up.

If you are exchanging contracts with an unrepresented third party, make sure that you either do so with a Nil deposit, or that any contract deposit is paid to the client account of another solicitor connected to the transaction, perhaps next up the chain, and who can give an undertaking to hold the money to order.

Practical Tip. If the other party in your transaction is not professionally represented, never send across to them draft documentation for approval, as you would to another conveyancer. In practice, it does not require any more work on your part to post across to them the final signature-engrossment, than it does to post something across to them in draft. What is important, is that they read and understand the document before signing and returning it to you.

If they come back to you with queries, you are still no worse off in terms of work-duplication. And of course, you have already warned them in writing to get independent legal advice before signing and returning the documentation. But there are some things which you need to tell the unrepresented party, like where to sign the document and that their signature has to be witnessed. And remember to pencil in the words, *'Do not date'* at the top of the document, so that you do not have the added problem of erasing an incorrect date when you are completing the transaction.

Professional Training

When the Law Society introduced a new requirement for all solicitors to undergo continuous professional development back in the mid-1980s, there was a restricted market for the delivery of such training. Most one-day CPD courses took place in hotel conference rooms at an average cost north of £350 pounds plus VAT. And that was at 1980's prices. But because the Law Society insisted that every solicitor, more than three years qualified, undertook a minimum 16 hours of professional development each practicing year, those solicitors had no choice but to pay what was demanded. And that was not the only cost, particularly for solicitors in private practice. There was also the loss of at day's fee-income.

First to break the mould was Professional Conferences, founded in 1992 by Michelle Tobias, which adopted an entirely new business model for the delivery of professional training.

Instead of hiring hotel conference rooms, Professional Conferences instead delivered their conferences in mass conference-venues, like Kensington Town Hall, which has an 828 person seating capacity in its Great Hall. Compare that with the 50 or so people who might be accommodated within a typical hotel conference room.

By achieving such economies of scale, Tobias was able to slash the cost of an individual attendance to something around £100 plus VAT. Even at today's prices, the costs have not increased significantly. Presenting to a mass audience also enables Professional Conferences to draw in sponsorship from conveyancing service-providers, including HM Land Registry, reducing the operating costs still further.

In fact, the only things on which Professional Conferences has never compromised on is the quality of their speakers, which compares favourably with those of more expensive conferences. But even with a reduced attendance-fee, there is still the hidden cost of a day's fee-earning, which will have been lost whilst you traipse through London. Such conferences also provide a great networking opportunity to engage with other legal professionals.

In the millennium years, the mould has been further broken with many barristers' chambers as well as blue chip solicitors firms offering free training seminars as part of a wider marketing strategy.

Those seminars, which may ranger either from an hour to an entire day, would focus on their core public sector clientel and on those specialist areas of law which that firm of chambers wishes to promote.

Many of these conferences are timed to take place outside core working hours and with the added bonus of post-presentation drinks and canapes as well as an opportunity to network with members of the team as well as other delegates, which might include some non-lawyers who could be considered as potential clients for the future.

A more recent change is the growth of on-line webinars, some of which are recorded, which means that you can attend those recorded webinars at the time which suits you. Attending a webinar means that you can probably fit it into your working day, without any noticeable loss of fee-income, but of course without the networking or the drinks or canapes.

There is now so much choice on how to go about meeting CPD obligations, which could involve a mix of face-to-face and online presentations. As a starting point, let's refer back to the current SRA requirements concerning continuing competence, which were last updated 9 August, 2022 .The SRA's opening statement says that all solicitors holding practising certificates must maintain their competence to carry out their role, which means that they must keep their professional knowledge and skills up to date. The guidance then referred back to the SRA's Competence Statement, which is that practising solicitors must: take responsibility for their personal learning and development; reflect on and learn from their practice and learn from other people; accurately evaluate their strengths and limitations in relation to the demands of their work; maintain an adequate and up to date understanding of relevant law, policy and practice; and adapt their practice to address developments in the delivery of legal services.

As part of the annual October practising certificate renewal, solicitors must confirm that they have identified learning and development needs in the previous year and that they have addressed these identified learning needs.

To meet continuing competence obligations, the SRA expects solicitors to: reflect (regularly consider the quality of their practice); identify (through reflection, identify their learning and development needs); plan and address (regularly update a plan on how they'll address their learning and development needs); record (keep an up to date record of their learning and development activity); and evaluate (think about the effectiveness of their learning and development).From the SRA guidance on continuing competence, it is possible to distil three key points:

- That the SRA the longer prescribes any particular method for keeping up to date. It is up to you and your team-leader to decide what works best for meeting the continuing competence requirement.
- The need to adopt a structured approach to assess what training requirements are needed to keep up to date with changes in the law and professional practice;
- Perhaps more critically, the need to keep a diary of all training courses which you have attended, including webinar presentations as well as internal courses delivered by your own organisation which are relevant to your work. In fact, it could be argued that every piece of specialist work you undertake concerning recent changes in the law, could be adding to your CPD. But only if you take the trouble to diary it up.

If you are primarily engaged in a specialist area of work, it is very easy to miss the wider changes that affect mainstream conveyancing practice. Even the free promotional courses offered by private firms of solicitors may not take you outside your specialist bubble. So a special effort has to be made to find those courses which deal with the mainstream of commercial and residential conveyancing.

Those type of courses are more likely to be paid-for courses because the organisation delivering them is not trying to promote their own expertise.

As we have seen, one option is to look out for appropriate Professional Conferences, which usually offer the option of attending online if you don't want to lose a day's work travelling to a conference venue. But there are also other options for keeping up to date with legal changes as well as practical innovations which relate to your work. Again, these options divide into the general and the specialist.

For general updates: make a point of reading through the Law Society Gazette, including the daily on-line updates. Amongst the legal chit-chat, there will also be important reference points relevant to your work, which may include links to important cases as well as updated guidance. Look out for the SRA bulletins, which mainly focus on anti-money-laundering. Sign up for a free online subscription to Today's Conveyancer.

This online bulletin is primarily aimed at private practice residential conveyancers and is mainly focused on the UK Property market but also provides updates of interest or to all conveyancers.

For the specialist updates most relevant your work, sign up to Local Government Lawyer, which is a weekly online bulletin aimed specifically at lawyers working in local government, not just conveyancers.

Amongst the public sector news and job opportunities, you will also find links to legislation, new government guidance and landmark legal decisions. Other online resources for local government lawyers include membership of Lawyers in Local Government, which again publishes weekly news letters. Perhaps most important of all is the need to take a personal interest in legislative changes, new legal guidance and case law, even where you do not consider it directly relevant to your day-to-day work.

Finally, please remember, that earning CPD points is not just about being a passive listener to presentations given by other people. You can also go part way to meeting CPD requirements by delivering presentations to colleagues and clients, or just by writing the occasional legal article, and raising your own professional profile in the process. So be prepared to share your wisdom with your clients and other legal colleagues. There is no better way to engage with clients and prospective clients.

5 OUTLINE OF A TRANSACTION

Not so long ago, a feature of every local authority conveyancing department was the large terrier map or, series of maps, either pinned to the wall, or hanging in a metal suspension cabinet.

Taken as a whole, this series of maps would cover the whole of the council's administrative area. Coloured in pink would be those areas of land and buildings owned by the local authority.

There might be separate colourings for other property interests, such as rights of way. Not only that, the deed packet numbers of each of these pieces of land would be overwritten in black ink on each of the red colourings, meaning that the title deeds for any piece of land could be found quickly and easily.

When land owned by the local authority was sold off, either on freehold or on lease, other delineations would be added to the map to alert anyone looking at it that the land had been sold off. As new land was acquired, fresh pink coverings and deed packet numbers would be added. But an old fashioned terrier map with its many hand written delineations has no place in a modern paperless office. Which is why, for most local authorities, those maps have now gone, along with the easy source of reference which they provided.

Their absence means that finding title deeds has now become much more of a hit and miss affair, particularly where title deeds are now often stored off-site, meaning that it is no longer possible to browse through racks of deed packets to try to find the particular package which you are looking for. That's progress!

The ability to sift through the contents of an original deed packet is important for any complex title investigation, even when you are dealing with a registered title. Because, even where the main freehold or long leasehold title is registered, there will often be some minor occupational or third-party interests which do not qualify for registration, such as leases for less than seven years or wayleaves. And there will always be some titles which slip through the net, even where there has been a comprehensive registration exercise.

We now look at the various steps involved in any local authority conveyancing transaction, whether it involves a purchase; a sale; a lease; or licence; or the grant of an easement. If we were to put this in the form of a checklist, it would contain the following elements:

- Who is the client?
- Who is the instructing-officer?
- What is the property?
- What is the client trying to achieve?
- What is your professional role in the transaction?
- Is there any conflict of interest?
- What executive authority exists for the transaction?
- What are the deadlines for exchange and completion?
- What are the risks of something going wrong or a client's expectation not being met? And what are the consequences if something goes wrong?
- Opening the file and acknowledging the instructions. Also notifying every other party to the transaction that you are the person who will be dealing with it(as well as the agent who negotiated the transaction).
- Checking the heads of terms.
- Setting up file alerts.
- Checking the title.
- Checking the other party and their legal representation
- When is a site inspection necessary?
- Setting up a process for exchanging contracts and completion.

- Determining what documentation is required and who should take responsibility for drafting it.
- Reporting back to clients before contracts are exchanged and again once the transaction has completed.
- Post completion work, including land registration where applicable and possibly filing a stamp duty land tax return.
- Dealing with file closure and return of documents.

Let's now take each of these in turn.

Who is the client?

We have already addressed the large number of clients for whom an in-house solicitor is permitted by SRA regulations to act. Particularly when the employer is a local authority.

In most cases your client will be the local authority for whom you are employed or contracted. But it is not as simple as that. With the exception of town and parish councils, any major local authority is conglomeration of many different public sector functions including: housing; town planning; public health; social services; parks and recreation, each with their own separate agendas and management structures, some of which pull against each other.

Maybe your local authority client is not even acting in its own right, but instead, in some other capacity, such as a charitable trustee or as the personal trustee of an individual not deemed legally capable of managing their own affairs, such as a minor or someone suffering from a mental impairment. In those last circumstances, the client is technically the beneficiaryof the trust, of which the council is the trustee, or the owner of the asset for whom the council is acting as trustee.

Who is the instructing-officer?

Any corporate entity is, for all practical purposes, a collection of individuals who speak corporately with one voice. In the case of a company, those individuals are the members of the company and the directors, to whom powers of management are delegated. In the case of a local authority, those individuals are the elected members of the authority and the senior officers of that authority to whom authority has been conferred to make decisions and issue instructions to subsidiary departments, such as legal services.

What is important for the conveyancer, is that there is clarity as to who is issuing instructions on behalf of the corporate client and that they had the seniority to issue those instructions. In some cases, those instructions may be subject to confirmation by someone having greater seniority in the department.

Generally, within each local authority service area, there will be someone with the authority to issue instructions to legal services on behalf of that service area.

What is the property?

In any conveyancing transaction, it is necessary to identify, with clarity, the extent and location of the property involved, preferably with a redline plan showing the extent of the property the subject of the transaction by reference to adjoining streets and other natural features. The property may have a postal address and postcode. Or it may just be a piece of land in the middle of nowhere. The property may be occupied or it may be vacant, or a mixture of the two.

Where there are multiple levels of ownership in the form of a freehold with a hierarchical leasehold structure, it is necessary to identify to which freehold or leasehold level of ownership, the transaction relates.

What is the client trying to achieve?

Client instructions should never be taken at face value. Client instructions require analysis to ascertain exactly what, strategically, the client is trying to achieve. It is about looking at the bigger picture.

Detailed client instructions should therefore be looked at critically to ascertain whether they will really achieve the client's objective or whether there is a better or more cost effective way in achieving those objectives. It is therefore important that the client is alerted, at the earliest moment if there are strategic issues with instructions or whether there may be a better way to proceed.

What is your professional role in the transaction?

Even where the substance of a transaction has been outsourced to a private firm of solicitors, you may still have a professional role as your client's in-house representative.

Unless your client's chief estate surveyor or other chief officer is dealing directly with that external firm of solicitors, someone from the in-house legal team may be called upon to manage the instruction from the client side. If that is the case, you will still be your client's first point of contact and provide the interface between your client and the external solicitors. In fact, you may even be involved in the engagement of that external firm of solicitors, which is a detailed piece of work in itself.

The process of engaging an external firm of solicitors to act for your corporate client will firstly involve you writing a specification of the legal work required, which will then become the starting point for any procurement exercise which is consistent with procurement law as well as your council's own contract standing orders.

One of the first questions to ask when instructing an external firm of solicitors is whether your council has membership of a legal framework, such as that hosted by the London Boroughs Legal Alliance (LBLA). Such frameworks will have already been through the statutory procurement process, which means, as far as you are concerned, that half the work involved in the firm-selection has already been done. It is then about selecting those solicitors firms on the framework who you consider best placed in terms of expertise and resource, to carry out the required tasks, and then to seek formal written quotations based on the service-specification which you have prepared.

Even where an external firm has been engaged to carry out the bulk of the conveyancing work, there are some areas of that work which only you, as the in-house representative, can deal with, such as drafting content for a delegated report to authorise the transaction.

Is there a conflict of interest?

Even where you are working for a single employer, there may still be conflicts of interest which need to be identified and managed. An obvious conflict may arise between the Planning Department which sometimes has to say 'no' to a prospective development, even where that development involves the council's own land or land which the council needs to acquire to deliver the maximum amount of affordable housing or further the council's economic interests.

The potential for conflicts of interest are even higher if the transaction is between the council corporately and an associated corporate entity, such as a council-controlled company or other organisation in which the local authority is a major stakeholder, even though that other organisation is not part of the internal corporate structure.

Having a modern electronic case management system makes it easier to identify actual or potential conflicts of interest by identifying other transactions relating the same property in which the council has been involved, not necessarily being other conveyancing transactions, but possibly relating to town planning or highway issues.

Where a conflict-of potential conflict of interest-has been identified, it is important that the potential conflict is logged on whatever case management system is used and a decision must then be made as to whether the conflict is such that some of the work has to be outsourced to a different firm of solicitors.

However, where there is a mutuality of interest, there is nothing intrinsically to prevent the internal legal service acting for both parties, so long as each party is treated as a separate client and, where necessary, a separate fee-earner is assigned to each party.

One issue which arises when you are acting for more than one client in a single transaction, even when the clients are associated with each other and there is mutuality of interest, is the need to maintain professional confidentiality.

It is perhaps another reason to appoint, from within the same legal team, separate fee-earners to represent each party. However, appointing a separate fee earner for each party does not have to mean duplication of work, provided that there can be agreement between those colleagues as to who does what.

If both fee earners are working within the same case management system, it is also important to ensure of that a separate file is opened up for each party and that the contents of each file are kept private to that fee earner.

What executive authority exists for the transaction?

Every body-corporate must have a constitutional process for making decisions. In the case of a company, that constitutional process comprises a mix of company law and regulation, which governs all registered companies, coupled with the memorandum and articles of association specific to that company, together with any delegations to individual directors or senior officers of the company which sit below the articles of association.

For any local authority, that constitutional process is contained within the written constitution which Section 9P of the Local Government Act 2000 (as amended) requires every local authority to maintain. *Section 9P(1) states:*

(1) A local authority must prepare and keep up to date a document (referred to in this section as a Constitution) which contains-
   a) a copy of the local authority's standing orders for the time being;
   b) a copy of the local authority's code of conduct (if any) for the time being under Section 28 of the Localism Act 2011;
   c) such information as the Secretary of State may direct;
   d) such other information (if any) as the local authority considers appropriate.

Section 9P also requires this constitution to be made available for inspection by elected members of the local authority as well as the wider public and a copy must be provided to any person who bequests a copy. In practice, many local authority constitutions can be downloaded in full from that council's public website.

One problem with many local authority constitutions is that they are not written with the legal precision of, say, a company's articles of association.

There are no model 'off the shelf' council constitutions as there are with company registration. Each local authority constitution is a bespoke democratic document, perhaps running into hundreds of pages, drafted by a cross-party working group of councillors and senior officers and approved by politicians.

Such documents are can be slow and difficult to navigate, particularly when trying to identify which council committee or chief officer is able to authorise a particular transaction. Where there is doubt, the arbiter in such situations will be the council's Monitoring Officer, who is the person with statutory responsibility under section 5 of the Local Government and Housing Act 1989 for reporting illegal activity relating to the council's functions and also with responsibility for the operation of the council's constitution.

Whilst a council's constitution sits beneath national legislation governing local authorities and their functions, it has to be assumed that the local constitution is consistent and fully compliant with those wider legislative requirements.

It means that the constitution can be treated as a stand-alone document which provides everything which a council's elected members and senior officers need to know to make valid and legally binding decisions.

Another key difference between local authority decisions and those of other corporate organizations, is that council decisions are generally in the public domain, save only where they are exempt from publication because they are either contain sensitive personal information or other information which can be regarded as commercially sensitive.

Like the constitution itself, most decisions of a larger local authority and its cabinet and committees, will be published online, including decisions made by chief officers pursuant to their delegations. Again, the exceptions will be those decisions which are exempt from publication on the grounds that they contain personal or other sensitive information.

For the local authority conveyancer, a key part of any local authority constitution are its contract standing orders (which may exist under different names), which govern the process to be followed when a local authority enters into any contractual arrangements with a third party. Well drawn contract standing orders will be fully consistent with national law relating to the award of public contracts as well as the physical process for getting legal documentation signed off.

It is those narrow parts of the constitution which will specify which documents need to be attested as a Deed and for which transactions a simple signature may suffice. It will also tell you what collateral security may be required to secure a contractor's performance of a high value contract.

It should also be possible to ascertain, from that constitution, who is eligible to sign off any legal document on behalf of the local authority, even if their job title has since changed. In fact, a significant source of Land Registry requisitions relating to local authority transactions, is the need to satisfy the Land Registry that the person's witnessing the affixing of the councils common seal, has the constitutional authority to do so.

Remember also that there may be some transactions where the local authority is not acting corporately on its own right but in some other capacity, perhaps as a charity trustee or in circumstances where an officer of the social services authority has been appointed by the Court of Protection to act as Deputy, to deal with the financial affairs of somebody who is adjudged incapable of managing their own affairs in circumstances where there is no next of kin or other appointee to take on that role.

What is important is that the required constitutional authority for a transaction is in place by the time contracts are exchanged, or if there is no contract, the date of completion.

In most cases, you will not even be able to get the documentation signed off by the local authority until there is evidence of a constitutional authority. However, it is possible that this constitutional sign off is not in place at the time you are first instructed. In those cases, it is necessary to flag up on the file the fact that the constitutional authority for the transaction has yet to be obtained. In fact, part of the added-value which you can provide as an in-house conveyancer, is to assist in drafting, for your client's approval, the content of the committee report or resolution or delegated reports, needed to get contracts are exchanged and the transaction completed.

What are the deadlines?

Some transactions have critical deadlines. Such as the statutory two-month deadline for serving the landlord's counter notice in response to a leaseholder's claim for freehold enfranchise and or lease extension.

A failure to meet that deadline means that the landlord will be deemed to have accepted whatever proposal the leaseholder has put forward for the buying out of the landlord's interest or lease-extension. Other deadlines may be less legally critical but will undermine client confidence in the team's ability to turn work around within a reasonable timescale. For example, a client's wish to meet a particular auction-date for the sale of the property.

Some deadlines will be driven by the negotiated heads of terms, with the possible collapse of a transaction if contracts are not exchanged by the stipulated date. Once contracts are exchanged, all contractual deadlines become critical. What is important then is that the appropriate file alerts are put in place to ensure that the deadline is not missed. This will include updating a team diaryso that colleagues are aware of the deadline if, for any unforeseen reason, you are not able to deal with the matter yourself.

For some complex property transactions, the dates for exchange of contracts and completion may not be the only critical deadlines. There may be other stages in between, particularly where the performance of their contract is made subject to other events, such as a grant of planning permission.

What are the risks of something going wrong?

With property transactions, perhaps more than anything else, time is money. Delay in completing a lease could mean a delayed rental stream. A delay in bringing a transaction to an exchange of contracts, could result in the transaction collapsing.

Some risks may be obvious from the start. Other risks may only become apparent as the transaction progresses, such as a title-discrepancy. Either way, the risk has to be logged and the client alerted, as soon as the risk becomes apparent.

Opening the file and acknowledging instructions.

Any client needs the confidence that someone within your team is dealing with their instruction. They will know that when they receive your e-mail acknowledging formal receipt of their instruction and providing your contact details.

Opening-up an electronic file also alerts everyone else in your team that progress on the transaction is in hand and that you are the person dealing with it.

Before opening-up a file on a new instruction, it is also important to ensure that there is no other file already existing on the same matter, including any previous files which have been closed. You may also find files relating to the same property but dealing with different issues, such as a section 106 planning agreement.

In opening the file, it is also important to import within the file everything which has been provided by your client or which you have obtained from other sources and that such documentation is, even at this early stage, correctly labeled up for future reference.

As well as the client, there may be other parties who need to be notified at the same time. These will be the legal firm representing the other party as well as any agent involved in the negotiation of the transaction.

Checking the Heads of Terms

Ideally, as the person dealing with the transaction, you would have been involved in the negotiation of the heads of terms before they are finally signed off between the parties. More often than not, that won't have happened.

Instead, you will receive an e-mail from the client attaching the heads of terms as negotiated together with such constitutional authority as exists to exchange contracts and completion the transaction. It is then about taking a critical due diligence review of those instructions and alerting your client to anything which you may consider to be problematic or where you consider that there may be a better way of achieving the same result.

It is those heads of terms, once agreed and signed off between the parties, which will provide the framework for the transaction. It is also the document you will use as a checklist to ensure that all of your client instructions have been fully met by the time contracts have been exchanged on a transaction or, where there is no contract, the transaction has proceeded straight to completion.

Setting up file alerts

File alerts should be part of the file-opening process. They give you (and anyone else looking at the file) advance warning of an approaching deadline. They should not only be apparent from the file itself but also in an electronic diary, including any team diary.

Checking the title

In the next chapter we deal with the detail of a typical local authority title investigation and the specific points which you need to look out for. In this section, we simply advise on the need to carry out that basic title check as soon as you have opened up your new file and imported basic downloaded title information on to that file.

The fact that most land in England and Wales is now registered, means that relevant title information can usually be identified and downloaded quickly. It is important at this stage to make sure that your local authority client has the necessary proprietary rights in the property to enter into the transaction and to flag up any potential title issues requiring further investigation.

If you are acting on the purchase of land from another party, don't wait for the other party's legal representative to send you title documentation if you are able to download it instantly from a land registry website and at minimal cost.

Checking the other party and of their legal representation.

If the other party is represented by a solicitor or licensed conveyancer based in the UK, you are entitled to assume that the legal representative has carried out the required 'know your client' due diligence when taking on that client. However, there are other due diligence checks which should be made at the outset of a transaction as regards every party to that transaction who is not already known to you.

If that other party is a company or limited liability partnership, registered in the UK, it is possible to carry out an instant check as regards the legal structure of the company or LLP, as well as its registered office, directors and company secretary (if any), as well as anyone having significant control of the company, by logging on to the Companies House website. That company information can also be summarised in the form of a company snapshot and imported to file.

Where the other party has charitable status, similar information can be downloaded from the Charity Commission website, which contains an open register of UK charities.

That information may not be so accessible where the other party is registered corporately under other legislation, such as registered societies. Additional due diligence will always be required where a company is registered abroad (including other UK Territories such as the Channel Islands; Gibraltar; or the Isle of Man, who are also regarded as foreign jurisdictions when it comes to conveyancing).

If the other party to your transaction is a company or other corporate organization registered outside the UK, it is necessary to have regard to the additional registration requirements set out in Land Registry Practice Guide 78, "Overseas Companies and Limited Liability Partnerships", which deals with the additional due diligence required in those cases.

Under the Economic Crime (Transparency and Enforcement) Act 2022, off-shore organisations owning land or intending to acquire land in the UK are required to join the Register of Overseas Entities, which is now maintained at Companies House.

This is in addition to any other due diligence required to ensure that documentation executed by the offshore entity is properly executed, which would, as a matter of course, include obtaining a written opinion from a lawyer practising in the jurisdiction and confirming that the organisation has power to enter into the transaction and that the documentation is properly executed in accordance with the laws of that jurisdiction.

Is the firm representing the other party known to you? If not, additional due diligence will be required to confirm the bona fides of the other conveyancer with which you are dealing. Remember, that it is not only clients who may be impersonated or are fictitious. Sometimes it is the other firm with which you may be dealing with, which is bogus. Information regarding all solicitors in England and Wales holding a practising certificate can be found through a due diligence SRA search.

When is a site inspection necessary?

One thing which can be guaranteed whenever you physically inspect property the subject of a conveyancing transaction, is that you will discover something which you didn't know previously.

It may be the existence of a manhole, suggesting the presence of underground services. Or a lamp column. In many cases, the property will look entirely different from the way you imagined it when looking at title documentation or the site plan provided by your client. Suddenly, everything is put into context. The transaction comes to life. It is about real land and buildings. And real people.

It is why, in any complex transaction, a visual inspection should form part of your title investigation, whether you are acting on the purchase or sale of a property. The existence of remote search-engines, such as Google Earth or Street View, means that a physical inspection may not always be necessary if you can see what you need to see from your computer laptop.

Setting up a process for exchanging contracts and completion.

If you do not have access to a solicitors' client account, you will need to think about the process you are going to adopt for transferring or receiving money both at exchange of contracts and on completion and ensure that there are specific provisions in the contract to deal with this.

This is because the Standard Conditions of Sale and the Standard Commercial Property Conditions, which govern almost all conveyancing transactions in England and Wales, pre-suppose that deposits and completion balances will be transferring between solicitors' client accounts.

But if you are working in-house for local authority, monies will not be transferred in this way. Instead any deposits or completion monies paid on the purchase will be coming straight out of your council's bank account to the client account of the receiving solicitor. Any capital receipts, whether of deposits or completion-balances, will be coming from the client account of the buyer's solicitor directly to the bank account of the local authority.

In neither case will you-the conveyancer-have any direct control over money is coming in or out of your local authority's account. But unless specific contractual provision is made to vary the way in which deposits or completion monies are paid or received, the solicitor acting for the other party will be under no obligation either to pay or accept transaction-monies other than to or from another solicitor's client account. It is why it must be clear from any contract for the sale of a property by your local authority client, that any capital-receipt is paid directly to your client.

Equally, any contract for the purchase of a property, must make clear that the deposit or completion monies will come direct from the account of your local authority client to the client account of the the solicitor acting on the sale.

For same reason, the standard contractual obligation requiring you to hold money as stakeholder will need to be varied, because you will have no account-facility even to hold money a stakeholder.

We now turn to the financial-mechanics of exchanging contracts or completing a transaction.

Because you have no direct control over money is paid or received by your local authority client, you cannot safely give any undertaking either to make a payment or to hold money to the order of another party. In practice, this mean that any contract deposit or completion monies must reach the client account of the receiving party solicitor before the contract exchange or completion takes effect. You are then reliant on their solicitor's undertaking to hold that money to your order before the associated exchange or completion actually takes effect. For the same reason, you cannot safely complete any transactional-disposal until you have received confirmation from your council's finance officer that the money has been safely received.

In both scenarios, you are relying on the goodwill of the other solicitor or licensed conveyancer to deal with the matters in the way you have requested. It is why such practical considerations cannot be left as an afterthought but must be written into the contract, or at least covered off in correspondence between lawyers, in good time before the transaction is scheduled to exchange or complete.

Mortgages

Dealing with the redemption of existing mortgages against a property are particularly problematic for an in-house conveyancer who does not have direct control over the transmission or receipt of funds.

Section 13 of the Local Government Act 2003 expressly prohibits any local authority from granting a mortgage over any of its assets. Any mortgage created by a local authority in breach of this prohibition is also rendered unenforceable as regards realisation of that security. It also means that the redemption of existing mortgages does not routinely form part of a local authority conveyancer's work. Although this statutory prohibition does not prevent local authorities taking the benefit of a mortgagee entered into by another party. But as always, there are exceptions. For instance:
1. The local authority takes ownership of a property the subject of an existing mortgage, which has yet to be discharged.
2. You are acting for a corporate subsidiary or associated company of your local authority employer, for whom the professional

rules allow you to act, and to whom the section 13 prohibition on mortgaging assets has never applied.
3. You are acting on the redemption of a mortgage charged on a property owned by another party but which is expressed to be for the benefit of your local authority client.
4. You are dealing with a deputyship sale or similar transaction in which your local authority client is acting as the trustee for property held in the name of a beneficiary and which is in mortgage to a third party lender.
5. You are acting in the forced sale of a property which is in mortgage to your local authority. Such a situation might arise where your local authority holds an express legal charge over a property to secure moneys payable or alternatively where the local authority holds a statutory charge, perhaps secured as a local land charge, which itself can take effect in as a charge by way of legal mortgage, though not actually enforceable until notice of that charge is transferred to the register of title, if the particular land is registered.

Although a local land charge takes effect in law as an 'overriding interest', section 55 of the Land Registration Act 2002 prevents enforcement of any statutory mortgage affecting registered land, until the statutory charge is actually registered against that title.

The fact that you, as the council's conveyancer, have no control over the transmission or receipt of funds by your employer, means that, for all practical purposes, you are not in a position to safely give any personal undertaking to redeem an existing mortgage from the buyer's completion monies. So you need to find a workaround.

First of all, it means amending the standard conditions in the contract so that you are not required to give a professionally binding to the other conveyancer when completing the transaction.

If the balance outstanding is small or negligible, the contract may allow you to utilise part of the contract deposit towards the discharge of that mortgage.

If the amount required to discharge the existing mortgage is significant, it may be impossible to deal with the entirety of the transaction 'in-house' at all. In those circumstances it may simply be safer to outsource the transaction to a private firm of solicitors with a client account, or at least that part of the transaction involving redemption of the mortgage. The contract terms will then require the purchase money to be transmitted directly to the client account of that firm of solicitors to enable discharge of the outstanding mortgage.

Again, if the organisation for which you are acting (which in these circumstances can't be your local authority employer), is taking out a new mortgages related to the transaction, it may again be easier and safer simply to outsource the entirety of that transaction to a private firm of solicitors.

Practice Point–remember the Companies Act requirement, now contained in the Companies Act 2006 (Amendment of Part 25) Regulations 2013, to register any charge created by a registered company with Companies House and within 21 days.

This 21-day limit is critical. Which means that you only have one chance to get it right. Which is why it will always be safer to register the document online, if you're able to do so, as it will enable you to pick up any registration errors immediately.

The only exception to this rule are rent deposits associated with a lease, for which there is specific exemption. Consider also whether this Registration Requirement will apply to statutory agreements entered into by a company pursuant to section 106 of The Town and Country Planning Act 1990; Section 16 of the Greater London Council (General Powers)Act 1974; or section 33 of the Local Government (Miscellaneous Provisions)Act 1982, in circumstances where any of these agreements include a future obligation to pay money, which can be registered as a local land charge and is then enforceable in the same way as if it had been created as a charge by way of legal mortgage.

In circumstances where a mortgaged property is occupied, it will always be necessary firstly to obtain a court order for possession, as a precursor to any forced sale taking place. However, even where a property is long-term vacant, or uninhabitable or in unknown or untraceable ownership, it is still necessary to serve notice on the mortgagor in accordance with section 103 of the Law of Property Act 1925, even if the notice has to be affixed to the land. Section 103 reads as follows:

Section 103 Regulation of exercise of power of sale.
A mortgagee shall not exercise the power of sale conferred by this Act unless and until—

(i) Notice requiring payment of the mortgage money has been served on the mortgagor or one of two or more mortgagors, and default has been made in payment of the mortgage money, or of part thereof, for three months after such service; or (ii) Some interest under the mortgage is in arrear and unpaid for two months after becoming due; or

(iii) There has been a breach of some provision contained in the mortgage deed or in this Act, or in an enactment replaced by this Act, and on the part of the mortgagor, or of some person concurring in making the mortgage, to be observed or performed, other than and besides a covenant for payment of the mortgage money or interest thereon.

Determining what documentation is required and who should take responsibility for drafting it.

By convention it is a seller's lawyer who drafts the initial contract for sale for despatch to the buyer's lawyer for approval. However, that does not work so easily with local authority conveyancing, particularly where special terms and conditions need to be included in the contract to make the mechanics of the transaction work, in circumstances where you do not have access to a solicitors' client account. Therefore, in most circumstances, it may be easier if you take responsibility for drafting that initial package of documentation, whether you are acting for the buyer or the seller.

Having a template contract, whichcan be quickly populated before emailing out to the other legal representative, also makes sense if the particular transaction does not exist in isolation but is part of a generic series of class of transactions of a similar type.

One exception will be where your corporate client is taking a new lease from another party, which needs to be consistent with every other lease in the building or on the estate and for which a template already exists. And other exception is where your corporate client is purchasing units on a wider development 'off plan', where there needs to be absolute consistency between each individual transfer or lease. Nor, where you are acting on the purchase, should you wait for the seller's lawyer to produce title documentation before putting pen to paper.

The fact that most title information is now so quick and easy to download from a Land Registry website, at minimal cost, means that this task can be undertaken the moment you have received instructions and opened up your electronic file. As always, there will be exceptions. Some titles may not be registered at all. Whilst other transaction documents may be exempt from registration because they are short term or do not create any legal estate or interest in land.

Digital Registration Service

A recent development has been the introduction of the Land Registry's digital registration service which, for all practical purposes, is a mini case-management system in which you input key information relating to a proposed purchase, which will facilitate the registration process as soon as the transaction has been completed and reduce the risk of a errors and Land Registry Requisitions.

When acting on a purchase of registered land (whole titles), our recommendation is that you should download existing title information and begin inputting data about the pending transaction, as soon as you have sufficient information to do so.

At that point, you will be given the option of self-generating a partially completed TR1, which can then be utilised in the transaction itself. Though, for reasons we do not understand, this self-generated TR1, which is only provided as a PDF, does not include a facility for inputting the relevant attestation clause, which means that this has to be added manually after the PDF has been produced.

Once you have inputted data on to the digital registration screen, you will then have up to 90 days to complete and register the finished transaction, before the data has to be re-uploaded. Then, after the transaction has completed and you have dealt with stamp duty land tax formalities, where applicable, you will return to the digital registration screen and upload the remaining registration documents and formally submit the digital registration application. At that point, the digital registration service will self-generate an electronic AP1, which can be saved to file and avoids the need for this to be prepared manually.

Reporting back to clients before contracts are exchanged and again once the transaction has completed.

The starting point for any significant property transaction is the negotiated heads of terms. This may be a long document running to several pages and setting out each detailed step of the transaction and the timetable for exchange and completion. In fact you may have even assisted in the drafting of that document.

Or it may be a one-page letter from an estate agent, copied to each party, and setting out the sale particulars. It is also those heads of terms which may form part of any committee or delegated decision authorising exchange of contracts and completion of the transaction. But matters really proceed as smoothly as the agreed heads of terms may suggest.

As the transaction progresses, issues may arise, which need to be addressed between conveyancing lawyers. So, at the point at which contracts are about to be exchanged, the client needs to have been kept fully informed as to the current state of the transaction, including any departures from the previously agreed heads of terms. In other words, you need to prepare a detailed transaction report for the client including copies of any key documentation which form the subject of the transaction.

Where the transaction involves a purchase of an estate or interest from another party, your transaction report will need to include a detailed report on title enclosing copies of any relevant title documentation.

Note that when drafting a report on title for a corporate client, many in-house conveyancers make the mistake of using a template, perhaps more suited to a high street firm of solicitors acting for a private client in a one-off transaction. Such high street clients might need a title report packed with template disclaimers and qualifiers. Your corporate client does not.

Transaction Reports

Your corporate client does not want key title information submerged between a raft of the disclaimers. Your client wants something which is to the point and enables them to see at a glance whether there are any issues relating to the title or the proposed transaction of which they need to be aware. Any such issues should be within the opening paragraphs of a transaction report.

As with any title report, your transaction report should detail what searches you have carried out as well as the results of those searches; as well as any title-constraints affecting your client's proposals for the property once purchased. Where there are third party constraints, such as title restrictions, your client would not only want to know that they exist but also how those issues can quickly be resolved.

Note that the type of transaction report recommended in this section is more than just a title report, which tells the client whether there is a good and marketable title. A transaction report, as its name suggests, addresses the wider transactional issues and summarises the substance of the contractual arrangement which the client is invited to enter into and any contractual risks involved for the project. It is about giving the client, in one place, everything which the client needs to know to make an informed decision on the transaction at the critical point when contracts are about to be exchanged. After that, there is no going back.

You will also report back to the client as soon as contracts have been exchanged, with a summary of the completion arrangements and again after the transaction has been completed, when you will also be sending across to the client scanned copies of all the relevant completion documentation.

You will also provide your client with any brought-forward alerts, such as the dates of any future rent reviews or other trigger-dates. After that, there may be stamp duty land tax and registration formalities. It is only when those post-completion formalities have been successfully concluded, that it is safe to close your file and arrange for the safekeeping of original hard copy documentation.

Post completion work, including land registration where applicable and possibly filing a stamp duty land tax return.

We have already touched on this in the last section. Any land transaction cannot be fully complete until the conclusion of relevant post-completion formalities, including stamp duty land tax (where applicable) as well as completion of registration (where applicable).

For most purchases and sales, the first step in this post-completion process will be to send the signed completion documentation to the solicitor acting for the other party. In rare occasions, there may also be other post-completion formalities, such as the need to formally notify a third party, such as a ground landlord; to register a financial charge at Companies House; or to register or a local land charge, each of which are dealt with in greater detail in a later chapter.

Dealing with file closure and return of documents.

This is the point at which the transaction has been completed as well as all post-completion formalities. You have already reported back to your client with copies of key documentation and any brought-forward alerts to which your client needs to be aware. So now, it is just about reviewing your electronic file for closure and returning any original hard copy documentation for safekeeping. But this should also be done in a way which enables original signed documentation to be quickly found if the need arises.

6 TITLE INVESTIGATION

The starting point for almost any property transaction involving the purchase, sale, or leasing of land is a due-diligence title investigation. The fact that most freehold and long-leasehold title information is now instantly downloadable from the Land Registry Portal means that you no longer have to wait for another party to provide you with copies of their own title information before you can get on with the drafting.

In fact, the most difficult task may be in identifying the correct title numbers and ensuring that no registered title information is overlooked. Provided you have a red-line plan which clearly identifies the location of the property in relation to neighbouring street-information and other natural features, the safest way to ensure that you have complete title information is by making a Land Registry Index Map search.

But if you need that information instantly, and have a postcode or reference to a known title number, the other way is to download a land registry map search. It is then about picking through the mass of title numbers thrown up on your map search and of trying to guess those particular title numbers most relevant your transaction. But not all title information is instantly downloadable.

There will always be some titles which, for whatever reason, have escaped registration, usually because there has been no actual dealing with the title within living memory.

But the main reason why registration may not be complete, is that leases not exceeding seven years and other minor interests are largely exempt from compulsory registration.

There may be other land-interests, such as utility wayleaves which, although technically registrable, have never actually been registered. It is why, on any disposal or on the grant of any other land-interest, it is always good practice to look for an original deed packet, just to see if there is anything inside which relates to the title but is not registered at the Land Registry.

For the same reason, if you have access to an electronic case management system, you may discover other files relating the same property, including files which have previously been closed.

Statutory devolution of title

The Local Government Act 1972, which swept away the old boroughs, as well as the older urban districts and rural districts across England and Wales, still represents the most important and far-reaching reform of local government in the post war years.

Greater London was largely untouched by the 1972 reorganisation, which took effect 1 April, 1974, only because London had been the subject of its own comprehensive reform of London government a decade earlier, when, as a result of the London Government Act 1963, the new London Boroughs were established on 1 April, 1965, to take over the assets and functions of the previous councils. Other far-reaching reforms introduced by the London Government Act 1963, included the abolition of the old London County Council as well as Middlesex County Council and the establishment of a new administrative entity known as Greater London, which encompassed not only the former administrative areas of Middlesex and the London County Council but also took in chunks of the neighbouring home counties, for which Greater London became the new administrative hub.

To replace the now abolished Middlesex and London County Councils, the 1963 Act set up the Greater London Council, to undertake those strategic county-functions which were assigned to it by statute.

Nor was the Local Government Act 1972 the last significant reorganisation of local government, although it continues to codify the basic framework of local government as it exists in England and Wales. On 1 April, 1986, and for political reasons, the Greater London Council was itself abolished by the Thatcher government and its functions transferred out to the 32 London Boroughs. It was then another 14 years, before there was a new single representative body for London in the form of the London Mayor together with the newly created Greater London Authority and Transport for London.

Sitting beneath the statutory abolition of the old local authorities and their replacement by new statutory bodies, is the subsidiary legislation, primarily to deal with the transfer of assets and liabilities, as well as regulatory functions from the old authorities to the new.

In recent decades there has also been a continuity of local government constitutional and boundary changes dealt with at a local level. One of the most recent changes has been the abolition of the former Buckinghamshire County Council as well as the four district councils, being Aylesbury Vale; Chiltern; South Bucks and Wycombe on 1 April 2020 and the transfer of their respective functions, assets and liabilities to the newly created Buckinghamshire Council, which now operates as a unitary authority.

The constitutional change was formalised by the Buckinghamshire (Structural Changes) Order 2019, made pursuant to the Local Government and Public Involvement to Health Act 2007. And we can be certain that the changes will continue into the future, particularly with a new government.

The only local authority which, so far, has been largely untouched by these comprehensive and ongoing constitutional changes, has been the Common Council of the City of London, whose medieval origins can be traced back to the common law.

All of this complicates the life of the local authority conveyancer, because it means that, in many cases, the corporate name on the title deeds will not be the same name as the council which currently owns the asset.

For example, unregistered land purchased in the 19th century for development as a workhouse, might now be used as a secondary school. Yet the named owner on the title deeds is still the 'Overseers of the Poor'. Even modern Land Registry records may still refer to properties being owned by those urban and rural districts which existed before their abolition on 1 April 1974 and the transfer of those properties by operation of law to the newly created counties and districts.

In many cases the process of tracking the devolution of a land title from the corporation named on the deeds to its modern equivalent will require more painstaking research. In the next paragraphs of this book we provide some general legislative reference points for any conveyancer embarking on this is journey:

- The London Authorities (Property etc) Order 1964. This order was made in consequence of the London Government Act 1963 which, with effect from 1 April, 1965, abolished the old London County Council and Middlesex County council and created the new administrative area of Greater London, which also took in those parts of the Home Counties which were closest to London. At the same time, the 1963 Act also abolished the old boroughs, urban and rural districts within the enlarged Greater London area and redistributed their functions and assets, by operation of law to one of the newly created London Boroughs as well as creating the new Greater London Council, which now had designated strategic functions across the whole of the Greater London area. It follows, that this 1964 Property Order remains the primary reference point when dealing with old unregistered or registered titles still recorded as belonging to one of the abolished local authorities but where title has since devolved, by operation of law to one of the newly created local authorities.
- The Local Authorities (England)(Property etc)Order 1973. This Property Order performs the same task as the 1964 London Property Order (see above) but this time as regards those local authorities, outside London, abolished by the Local

Government Act 1972, and whose functions and assets and liabilities were transferred by operation of loss to the newly created counties and districts.

- The Local Government Reorganisation (Property etc) Order 1986. This property order was made in consequence of the Thatcher government's abolition of the former Greater London Council and other metropolitan Boroughs and the transfer of their functions to other Boroughs. In the case of London, functional property was transferred from the former GLC to the respective London Boroughs, with any residual assets or liabilities being transferred either to the newly created London Residuary Body or to the London Borough of Bromley, which had been nominated to sweep up any residual assets and liabilities which had not otherwise been allocated.
- The Local Government Reorganisation (Property etc) Order (No 2)1986. Following the setting up of joint waste disposal authorities by The Waste Regulation and Disposal Authorities Order 1985, this number No 2 Order deals with the transferor of assets and liabilities to the new waste disposal bodies.

As we have seen with the recent merger of the Buckinghamshire local authorities into a single unitary council, the reorganisation of local government is now a continuous and ongoing process, in which many local councils have been placed in direct competition with each other as each tries to justify its own continued existence. It is also correct to say that there are some older titles which had been the subject of successive devolutions of title, even predating the establishment of modern local government by the Local Government Acts 1888, 1894 and 1899.

So, for example, a public park still registered in the name of the former Middlesex County Council, may have transferred on 1 April, 1965, to the newly created Greater London Council. Then on 1 April 1986, there would have been a further statutory devolution from the now abolished Greater London Council to one of the individual London Boroughs, in whose area the park is situated.

A common mistake is to think that the Greater London Authority, established by the Greater London Authority Act 1999 (along with the Mayor for London and Transport for London), is the immediate statutory successor to the former Greater London Council. It is not. There was a gap of more than 16 years between the abolition of the former GLC on 1 April 1986 and the establishment of the GLA on 3 July, 2000, during which time London had no single public face.

For most assets and functions, the immediate statutory successor to the former GLC is the 32 London Boroughs, depending on where the land is situated. There is no statutory connection between the former GLC and the current GLA, which is entirely a new creation.

Gaps in the Title

Many large development sites comprise an amalgamation of many registered titles acquired piecemeal by the local authority, and its statutory predecessors, many years previously at the time the estate was previously redeveloped, perhaps for housing. But now that housing estate has reached the end of its useful life and is now part of a comprehensive regeneration scheme. You have carried out your initial due diligence title-check but note that amongst the amalgamation of local authority titles, there are gaps in which the council has no apparent documented ownership. In some cases, these may be shown as white spaces on any Land Registry Map Search, indicating that it has never been the subject of any application for registration. In other cases, part of the title may be shown is registered in the name of another party.

In most cases, there will be explanations for these title-anomalies, which may only become apparent after an extensive research. In the meantime we look at some of those explanations as to why those white spaces exist on your Land Registry Map Search. Here are some examples:

1. The council owns the land but it is never been the subject of any first registration of title. So it is then a matter of trying to find those deeds and documents and applying to the Land Registry for first registration of that title.
2. The registered boundary of one title does not marry up exactly with the boundary of an adjoining title, leaving slithers of unregistered land between the two titles. This does not mean that the council does not own that slither of land between the two registered titles, particularly where the two adjoining titles are registered in the council's name. Even more so where the council had always treated the land is its property and there is no obvious evidence of it belonging to someone else. The explanation is that the Land Registry operate a 'general boundaries rule', which means that the boundaries shown on the registered title plan may not follow the exact natural features of the land. However, it is possible to apply the Land Registry to declare a specific boundary line between the two properties.
3. With the exception of ancient highway and natural river beds, almost all land will at one time have been in someone's documented ownership. And this will include estate roads and alleyways, even for estates developed in the Victorian era, which pre-dated modern land registration. Those old estate roads and alleyways will likely be shown as 'white', on your Land Registry map search, only because there has been no change in ownership of those estate roads and alleyways since the development of the estate when the first plots were sold off. Without evidence of a documented title to such estate roads and alleyways between properties, it is necessary to apply legal presumptions as regards ownership of the subsoil, namely that the frontagers on either side of the road own the subsoil up to the centre

line. Sometimes a channel of land running through an estate will be marked 'white' on a Map Search because it comprises the subsoil of a previous highway which had been stopped up, using statutory powers, to enables an earlier redevelopment to take place. Then, it is about applying to the Land Registry to close those gaps by registering the ownership of the current or former highway in the council's name on the basis of those legal presumptions.

4. Ancient highways and river beds will rarely have been subject to any formal registration process or documented title, and proof of ownership will rely entirely on the legal presumptions relating to ownership of riparian rights as well as the subsoil of that ancient highway.

5. Where land is shown as being registered in the name of a third party but has for many years been treated as being within the council's ownership and maintained by the council as such, it may be a case of applying to the Land Registry for registration of title by adverse possession. But remember that under Schedule 6 of the Land Registration Act 2002, any registered landowner now has a one-off opportunity to veto an application for first registration by another party, so long as the possessory title had not already been obtained before the statutory changes took effect. In some cases, land may continue to be registered in the name of a company which has long since been dissolved and whose residual estate would and then passed to the Crown by bona vacantia, where a 30 year limitation rule would then apply.

6. In some cases, a registered title will refer to freehold land which is registered in the name of the local authority but subject to a registered lease or other third party interests, for which no other information is

available. Conversely, the council's own title may not be freehold but comprised within the residue of say a 999 year lease granted many years ago from by a freehold which is now in unknown ownership.
7. On most large housing estates, some individual houses and flats would have been sold off over the years under statutory right-to-buy and may have to be repurchased to enable the council to put its scheme into effect.

Whilst in many cases it will be possible to resolve title issues, in other cases, where there is perceived to be minimal actual risk, it will usually be possible to deal with the unresolved title issues by way of title Indemnity Insurance, which can usually be obtained at an affordable cost where the actual risk of a third party coming forward in the future to claim their rights is perceived as a negligible.

Statutory constraints affecting publicly owned land

All land owned by a local authority is owned for a specific statutory purpose. It would have been statute which authorised the original purchase of the property for public purposes, even if the local authority which originally acquired the property has long since been abolished and its functions transferred to other statutory bodies as part of a local government reorganisation. Or alternatively if the statute which authorised that original purchase has been long-since wiped from the statute book and superseded by later legislation. Nor does it mean that the original statutory purpose for which the land was publicly acquired is frozen in time.

Local authorities no longer need to acquire land to build workhouses. But they do need land on which to build schools, which is why land originally acquired in the mid 19th century by the 'Overseers of the Poorer', might now be used as a sixth form college..

Sometimes, the purpose for which the land was originally acquired will be apparent from documented title. A common restriction on many older local authority titles might read:

"Except under an Order of the Registrar no disposition by the proprietor of the

land is to be registered unless made in accordance with the Housing Act 1957 or some other act or authority."

You wouldn't find a modern restriction worded like that. Not least because the Housing Act 1957 has since been superseded by the Housing Act 1985.

Nor is the onerous, as it is not restricted to the old Housing Act 1957) but simply flags up the fact that it is publicly owned land originally acquired for housing purposes which cannot be sold or leased or except where there is statutory authority to do so.

So before proceeding further with the transaction, you need to identify the modern statutory authority for that transaction and ensure that it is written into the transfer, lease or other grant, so that it does not lead to any later objection or requisition from the Land Registry, when it comes to registration.

Other historic restrictions may require further investigation. Take for instance, the following restriction found on a registered title dating back to 1949.

"Except under an Order of the Registrar no disposition by the proprietor of the land is to be registered unless made in accordance with the Middlesex County Council Act 1944."

You might even have difficulty locating a copy of the Middlesex County Council Act 1944, to discover what the restriction is about. Apart from the fact that the Middlesex County Council was itself abolished by the London Government Act 1963, when its functions were devolved to other public bodies. It is an issue which we deal with later in this chapter.

When dealing with an existing local authority title, the starting point, apart from the title investigation itself, is to identify the statutory purposes for which the land is currently being held for. What is stated on the title may provide for a clue as to the authorised use of the land, but it is not conclusive. Being able to identify within which particular statutory regime public land is held is important because it will determine how the land can be used and what constraints affect the council's ability to sell, lease, or grant rights to any third party, as regards the whole or any part of the land comprised within that title.

The following criteria are relevant in determining within which statutory regime the land exists and, accordingly, what statutory constraints apply to its use or to any sale, or leasing or grant of third-party rights:
1. The statutory purposes for which the land was first acquired, if apparent from the documents of title;
2. How the land is currently actually being used;
3. Whether there is a record of any formal appropriation of the land from one statutory regime to another statutory regime and how that appropriation was formalised.

We start with a list of the main statutory categories of publicly owned land and how they affect a council's ability to sell, appropriate, lease or grant rights to a third party:

Housing Act 1985

As we have seen, the Housing Act 1985 is a statutory successor to the former Housing Act 1957 and is now the principal legislation under which local housing authorities operate when exercising their housing functions. Land and buildings falling within the 1985 Act will fall within a Council's Housing Revenue Account, or HRA, which is a ring-fenced account for a council's social housing stock and other land associated with that housing stock, such as garaging or greenspace.

It is to distinguish it from land held in a council's 'general fund' or specifically for a different statutory purpose. When it comes to any intended sale or leasing of HRA land, we have to start with Section 32 of the Housing Act 1985 which, in its amended form, states:

32 *Power to dispose of land held for the purposes of this part.*
(1) Without prejudice to the provisions of Part V (the right-to-buy) a local authority has power by this section, and not otherwise, to dispose of land held by them for the purposes of this Part.
(2) A disposal under this section may be effected in any manner but, subject to subsections (3) and (3A), shall not be made without the consent of the Secretary of State.

(3) *No consent is required for the letting of land under a secure tenancy or an introductory tenancy or under what would be a secure tenancy but for any of paragraphs 2 to 12 of Schedule 1 (tenancies other than long leases and introductory tenancies, which are not secure)*

(3A) *[this subsection relates only to Wales]*

(4) *For the purposes of this section only, the grant of an option to purchase the freehold of, or any interest in, land ,is a disposal and a consent given to such disposal extends to a disposal made in pursuance of the option.*

(5) *Sections 128-132 of the Lands Clauses Consolidation Act 1845 (which require surplus land first to be offered to the original owner and to adjoining land-owners) do not apply to the sale by a local authority of land held by them for the purposes of this Part.*

(6) *The Secretary of State shall consult the Regulator of Social Housing before deciding whether to consent under this section to anything within the Regulator's remit.*

Without more, it would be necessary for an application to be made by the Secretary of State under section 32 of the 1985 Act for any sale or leasing of HRA land, with the exception of statutory right-to-buy and the granting of residential tenancies.

For this reason, Section 32 has to be read together with the General Consent for the Disposal of Land held for the purposes of Part 2 of the Housing Act 1985 – 2013, which was issued pursuant to Section 34 of the 1985 Act,and which avoids the need to apply to the Secretary of State for express written consent in circumstances where the General Consent applies. For all practical purposes, the most important of the 2013 General Consents are A.3.1 and A.3.2, which are explained as follows:

A.3.1 Gives blanket approval for any sale at full market value of land and buildings which are not currently tenanted;

A.3.2 Gives blanket approval for the sale of vacant land, which is widely defined to include any HRA land on which no dwelling house is being built or, where a dwelling house had previously been built, that house has since been demolished or is now incapable of human habitation and is due to be demolished. Note that the main difference between A.3.1 and A.3.2 is that in the latter, it is not necessary to demonstrate that full market value has been obtained, as will be the case if the sale relied on A.3.1. In that respect A.3.2 is less onerous than the equivalent power of sale contained in section 123 of the Local Government Act 1972 (see below) which presumes that any land sold or leased under the 1972 Act will be on full market terms.

Local Government Act 1972

Any land belonging to a local authority, which does not fit into any other specific function-category will, by default, fall within the generic provisions of the Local Government Act 1972.

Section 120 of that act gives principal councils (being counties, districts and unitaries) a general power to acquire any land for a functional purpose. This would suggest that the Section 120 power of acquisition runs alongside and supports other functional legislation, perhaps filling a legislative gap, where that other functional-legislation does not deal in sufficient detail with the acquisition and disposal of land related to that function.

The sale or leasing of council owned land, which is not addressed in specific terms by other legislation, is covered by section 123 and section 123(2A) of the 1972 Act, which allows for the sale of land no longer required for a functional purpose at the best consideration reasonably obtainable.

In general, the consent of the Secretary of State is only required if the land is to be sold at below market value, and only then if it is a freehold interest which is being sold or a leasehold interest for more than seven years.

When assessing market value for the purposes of section 123, it is both legitimate and appropriate to look at the transaction as a whole, including any restrictions appropriately imposed on the buyer of the land, in particular where the land is being transferred for the development of affordable housing, which will be made available to nominees on the council's waiting list, and will mean that the value of the land, to the purchaser, is much less than if the land was sold on the open market on an unrestricted basis.

Even where land is being transferred or leased on the open market terms, statutory advertisement under section 123 (2)(A) of the 1972 Act is required if the land to be sold comprises a park or an area of public open space.

In circumstances where section 123 (2)(A) applies, the local authority intending to sell the land must first advertise the proposed sale in a local newspaper for two successive weeks and then give due consideration to any responses received to those advertisements.

Provided that this statutory formality has been complied with before the sale takes place, the land will be freed from by any public trust to which it may have previously been the subject, including the statutory trust created by section 10 of the Open Spaces Act 1906.

As well as applying to land held under the Open Spaces Act 1906, the requirement to advertise also applies to any land in the nature of a park or pleasure ground acquired under the Public Health Act 1875.

Whilst these administrative requirements are not onerous, it was held by the Supreme Court in R *(on the application of Day) (Appellant) v Shropshire Council (Respondent) [2023] UKSC 8*, that the consequence of failing to advertise was serious, as the failure meant that the statutory trust would not be extinguished and that the land is therefore incapable of being developed in the way proposed.

As is usual in this type of case, what really mattered to the parties was the validity of the grant of planning permission issued by Shropshire Council for the development of part of Greenfields Recreation Ground for the building of houses. Shrewsbury Town Council, the previous owner of the land, had sold the land to CSE Development (Shropshire) Limited in October 2017.

However, because of a mistake, the intended sale of the land had not been advertised under section 123(2)(A), because it had been thought wrongly that the land was not open space to which the legislation applied.

Dr Day, with other local residents, brought judicial review proceedings challenging the validity of the planning permission for the small housing development, arguing, amongst other things, that the existence of the trust is a material factor to which Shropshire Council, should have, but failed to have, regard within the meaning of section 70(2)(c) of the Town and Country Planning Act 1990, when considering whether to grant planning permission for the proposed development. His challenge succeeded.

Surprisingly, the Supreme Court also ruled that CSE Development (Shropshire) Limited were not protected by section 128(2) of the Local Government Act 1972 (consents to land transactions by local authorities and protection of purchasers) which states:

> *(2) Where under the foregoing provisions of this Part of this Act or under any other enactment, whether passed before, at the same time as, or after, this act, a local authority purport to acquire, appropriate or dispose of land, then-*
>
> *(a) in favour of any person claiming under the authority, the acquisition, or appropriation or disposal so purporting to be made shall not be invalid or by reason of any consent of a minister which is required thereto has not been given or that any requirement as to advertisement or consideration of objections has not been complied with, and*
>
> *(b) a person dealing with the authority or a person claiming under the authority shall not be concerned to see or enquire whether any such consent has been given or whether any such requirement has been complied with.*

Yes –the validity of the sale was protected by section 128(2). The only snag was that the land which the development company had acquired was still subject to a statutory trust keeping the land open and available for public access.

Local Government Act 1972 – General Disposal Consent 2003

Like the general consent issued under section 32 of the Housing Act 1985, referred to above, there is also a general consent under Section 123,enabling the disposal of land at an undervalue subject to compliance with a detailed administrative process involving red-book valuation. This is contained in the general consent forming the Annex to the Office of Deputy Prime Minister (ODPM) Circular 06/03 Local

Government Act 1972 General Disposal Consent (England) 2003. Disposal of land for less than the best consideration that can reasonably be obtained. The general consent itself, comprised within the annex to the circular reads as follows:

Annex

The Local Government Act 1972: General Disposal Consent England 2003

1. *The First Secretary of State (the Secretary of state) in exercise of the powers conferred by sections 123(2), 127(2) and 128(1) of the Local Government Act 1972 hereby gives consent to a disposal of land otherwise than by way of a short tenancy by a local authority in England in the circumstances which are set out in paragraph 2 below.*
2. *The specified circumstances are:*
    (a) *The local authority considers that the purpose for which the land is to be disposed is likely to contribute to the achievement of any one or more of the following objects in respect of the whole or any part of its area, or of all or any persons resident or present in its area: (i) the promotion or improvement of economic well-being; (ii) the promotion or improvement of social well-being; (iii) the promotion or improvement of the environment well-being; and*
    (b) *The difference between the unrestricted value of the land to be disposed of and the consideration for the disposal does not exceed £2,000,000(two million pounds).*
3. *In a this instrument, "local authority" means: (i) London Borough Council (ii) a county council (iii) a district council (iv) a parish council and parish trustees acting with the consent of a parish meeting (v) a national park authority(vi) a metropolitan borough council (vii) a joint authority established under Part IV of the Local Government Act 1985 (viii) a police authority*

>established under section 33 of the Police Act 1996;(ix) the Metropolitan Police Authority.

The following paragraphs of the circular itself provide further explanation as to how the general consent is intended to work and as to the process which local authorities are expected to follow when utilising the general consent

8. The terms of the consent mean that specific consent is not required for the disposal of any interest in land which the authority considers will help to secure the promotion or improvement of the economic, social or environmental well-being of its area. Where applicable, authorities should also have regard to their community strategy. Although these criteria derive from the Local Government Act 2000, their use in the consent is not confined to authorities with duties and powers under that Act. Therefore, authorities not covered by the 2000 Act can also rely upon the well-being criteria when considering disposals at less than best consideration. It will be for the authority to decide whether these decisions taken comply with any other relevant governing legislation. In all cases, disposal at less than best consideration is subject to the condition that the undervalue does not exceed £2,000.000 (two million pounds).

9. In determining whether or not to dispose of land for less than the best consideration reasonably obtainable, and whether or not any specific proposal to take such action falls within the terms of that consent, the authority should ensure that it complies with normal and prudent commercial practices, including obtaining the view of a professionally qualified value as to the likely amount of the undervalue.

10. It will be for the local authority to decide whether any proposed disposal require specific consent under the 1972 Act, since the Secretary of State has no statutory powers to advise authorities that consent is needed in any particular case. Once an application for a specific consent is submitted, the Secretary of State is obliged to make a decision on the proposed disposal on its merits. However, if he is of the opinion that his consent is not required (ie the sale is not at an undervalue), or if he believes that the case falls within the terms of the consents, his statutory function to give specific consent will not arise. Where an authority is uncertain about the need to seek consent, it may wish to seek its own legal advice on the matter. An authority might find it useful to keep its appointed auditor informed of any legal advice it receives and the proposed action it wishes to take. An auditor has a duty to consider whether the authority is acting lawfully.

11. Applications for specific consent should be sent to the Secretary of State via the Director of Planning at the Government Office for the relevant region. The Secretary of State will require the following information: (i) a written description of the site and its buildings, its physical characteristics, location and surroundings together with a plan which should be accurate enough to allow it to be used to identify the land in the Secretary of State's decision in cases where consent is given; (ii) a written description of the authority's tenure and a summary of the details of any leases, encumbrances, such as a easements etc., to which it is subject. Details should be given for the purposes for which the authority holds the land. Normally land is held for the purposes of the power under which it was acquired, or taken on lease, unless it has since been formally appropriated to another purpose;(iii) a written description of the existing uses, current planning consents and alternative planning uses that are likely to be permitted; (iv) a summary of the proposed transaction, noting the reasons for disposing at an undervalue, the key terms and any restrictions to be imposed by the authority; and (v) a detailed valuation report covering the matters listed in the technical appendix and signed by a qualified value (a member of the RICS). The department would normally expect the valuation to have been undertaken not earlier than six months before the submission.

(12) It is the responsibility of the authority to undertake any further procedures which may be necessary to enable it to dispose of any particular area of land. For example, Sections 123(2A) and 127(3) of the Local Government Act 1972 [see above] and Section 233(4) of the Town and Country Planning Act 1990 ("the 1990 Act") require a local authority wishing to dispose of open space under those powers to advertise its intentions in a local newspaper for two consecutive weeks and to consider objections. Authorities should carry out these procedures before making any final decisions about disposal as the public response to the notices may be material to any such decision. It could also be an important factor in any determination by the Secretary of state on an application for specific consent.

13. It is the responsibility of the authority to satisfy itself that the land is held under powers which permit it to be disposed of under the terms of the 1972 Act and, if not,

to take action to appropriate (for example under Section 122 of the 1972 Act). In this regard, authorities are reminded that the terms of the consent do not extend to proposals to dispose of land under section 233 of the 1990 Ac,t for which specific consent is still required. Nor does the consent apply to the disposal of land held under powers derived from the Housing Act 1985, upon which authorities should seek advice from LAH5 division in the Housing Directorate, ODPM, Zone 2D2, Eland House, Bressenden Place, London, SW1E 5DU.

14-16 Provide warnings about the need to consider the implications of State Aid on any sale at an undervalue. These particular paragraphs have been superseded following the UK's withdrawal from the European Union and the substitution of other provisions.

17. Before disposing of any interest in land for a price which may be less than the best consideration reasonably obtainable, local authorities are strongly advised in all cases to ensure that they obtain a realistic valuation of that interest, following advice provided in the Technical Appendix (see below). This applies even for disposals by means of formal tender, sealed bids or auction, and irrespective of whether the authority considers it necessary to make an application to seek the Secretary of State specific consent. By following this advice, an authority will be able to demonstrate that it has adopted a consistent approach to decisions about land disposals by carrying out the same step by step valuation process on each occasion. Supporting documents will provide evidence, should the need arise, that an authority has acted reasonably and with due regard to its fiduciary duty.

18. Where an authority wishes to grant an option, or an option holder wishes to exercise his option on land which the authority holds, the authority will need to consider whether the consideration for either the grant or exercise of the option will result in a discount. In relation to the exercise of an option, this will depend on the valuer's assessment of whether, if the option were to be exercised, the terms would be likely to require the authority to accept less than the best price that could reasonably be obtained for that interest at the time of disposal and, if so, whether that would fall within the terms of the consent. The matters which would need to be considered by the valuer are covered in paragraph 20 and 21 of the Technical Appendix. If, as a result of the valuer's advice, the authority wished to seek specific disposal consent, it would need to provide the Secretary of state with the full details of the terms of the option agreement which is to be entered into or implemented.

Note that the Technical Appendix refers to the 24 paragraphs appended to the end of the Circular which is headed "Valuation for the Purposes of Determining Whether Proposed Land Disposals under the terms of the Local Government Act 1972 fall within the provisions of the General Disposal Consent 200" and which deals with the matters to be a addressed within a professional valuation prepared to evidence the amount of an undervalue to evidence whether a particular intended disposal will be sufficiently covered by the terms of the general disposal consent.

Town and Country Planning Act 1990

Section 226 of the Town and Country Planning Act 1990 (compulsory acquisition of land for development and other planning purposes) (summarised) allows a local authority, on being authorized by the Secretary of State, to acquire by compulsory purchase any land in their area, if either:

(a) the authority think that the acquisition will facilitate the carrying out of development, redevelop and or improvement on or in relation to the land, or

(b) which is required for a purpose which it is necessary to achieve in the interests of a proper planning of an area in which the land is situated.

But section 226 (1A) prevents a local authority from exercising his power in relation to subsection (a) above unless they think that the development, redevelopment or improvement is likely to contribute to promote or improve the economic, social or environmental well-being of their area.

Section 226 (3) then gives the local authority additional power, on been authorised by the Secretary of State, to acquire by compulsory purchase any adjoining land required for the purposes of executing works related to the development or use. Subsection (4) makes clear that it is immaterial by whom the activity or purpose is carried out or achieved. However, the powers of acquisition contained in section 226 only relate to counties, districts and unitaries in England and not to towns or parishes.

Section 227 of the Town and Country Planning Act 1990 gives councils the same powers to acquire, by agreement, any land to which they would be authorised to acquire by compulsory purchase under section 226.

It is therefore clear that the acquisition of land pursuant to sections 22 6 or 22 7 of the 1990 Act has to be development-related and that there is also strict criteria which the decision-maker has to address before authorising acquisition under either of these sections. However where the statutory criteria is satisfied and the land is required for development purpose, purchase under sections 226 or 227 should be preferred to other statutory powers, because it engages other statutory provisions which can override certain third party interests which might otherwise impede development for which planning permission has been obtained, by converting those rights into a statutory right to compensation. This power to overrides third party rights is considered in greater detail in a later chapter.

Section 233 of the Town and Country Planning Act 1990 deals with the sale of land held for planning purposes and large the mirrors the general power of sale contained in section 123 of the Local Government Act 1972, in that or any sale must be at the best market terms. However, unlike section 123 of the 1972 Act, there is no general consent authorising sales at an undervalue, which means that an express application to the Secretary of State must be made before there can be any such sale below market value.

Education Land

School playing fields, in particular, have special protection under Section 77 of the School standards and Framework Act 1998 (control of disposals or change in the use of school playing fields) which, in summary, requires the consent of the Secretary of State before the disposal of any school playing fields which are currently being used by any maintained school or which have been so used at any time within the previous 10 years. However express Secretary of State consent is not required in any case where the School Playing Fields General Disposal and Change of Use Consent (No 7) applies, and which are summarised below:

Paragraph 4 of the document gives general consent to the disposal or change of use of playing fields, where the disposal or change of use is of a description specified in the Schedule to the General Consent, which are listed below:

1. *The disposal of an interest in land where an Academy Order has effect in respect of a maintained school which uses the land and the school is to be an academy (including: free schools, studio schools and universities or technical colleges).*
2. *The disposal or appropriation of an area of land less than 50 square metres, where such land is required for the purposes of are either: (a) constructing, maintaining or servicing a highway; or (b) health and safety requirements; (c) enabling the provision of gas, water, electricity or broadband, subject in any of these cases to the school supporting the proposal.*
3. *A disposal involving the granting of a leasehold interest in the whole school site, including the playing fields, to facilitate an existing agreement under a private finance initiative, provided there is no net loss of school playing fields.*
4. *A temporary disposal or change of use of a school playing field provided that: (a) the temporary disposal or change of use is for no longer than three school terms; (b) the Secretary of State is satisfied that the school is still able to deliver the curriculum to at least the same extent as it was able to pre-disposal or change of use; and (c) the applicant has provided written confirmation to the Secretary of State that the land will be returned to at least the same condition as it was beforehand.*
5. *The disposal of playing fields to a not-for-profit organisation when the following conditions are met:*
    (a) The terms of the disposal agreement provide that any school or community user group using the playing fields in the six months immediately before the transfer may continue to do so for at least 10

years following the date of the disposal, during which time they will have access to the playing fields for at least the same periods and on the same, or more favourable, terms as it did before the disposal; and either

(b) *The constitution of the receiving organisation obliges that organisation to maintain them as playing fields; or*

(c) *The terms of the disposal agreement require that organisation to maintain them as playing fields for at least 10 years from the date of disposal; or*

(d) *The disposal is to a local authority and the receiving authority has given an undertaking that the playing fields will continue to be used as school/community playing fields for at least 10 years from the date of disposal.*

6. *The disposal of hard play areas and enclosed social areas and other ancillary social and recreation or habitat areas that surround the buildings and closed or closing school sites provided that either: (a) no other schools share the whole or any part of the site; or (b) the body seeking to dispose of the land can satisfy the Secretary of State that the areas in question are not needed by any other schools which share or boarder the site. In relation to this particular consent, 'hard play area' means an incidental recreation area with tarmac, concrete or paved surfaces and does not include areas provided mainly for any type of sport.*

7. *The grant of an easement and/or the wayleaves over playing fields where such land is required for the purpose of either: (a) constructing, maintaining or servicing a highway; or (b) health and safety requirements; or (c) enabling the provision of gas, water, electricity or broadband —subject in any case to the school supporting the proposal.*

8. *The disposal or change of use of playing fields where, upon that disposal or change of use, any school which used to the original playing fields in the six months immediately before that disposal or change of use, will have made available to it, replacement playing fields, provided that all the following requirements are met: (a) the replacement playing fields are of at least the same area as the original playing fields; (b) the replacement playing fields are capable of sustaining 7 hours use a week per school that will have use of those playing fields (c) be replacement playing fields are immediately available to any schools which used the original playing fields on the same,*

or more favourable terms as the original playing fields had been; (d) the replacement playing fields have the same or better standards of facilities as the original playing fields; (e) the location of the replacement playing feels is such that the schools using them are able to carry out the curriculum to at least the same standardas they were on the original playing fields (f) the replacement playing fields do not comprise land at open schools and (g) there is no reduction in the amount or types of sports provision currently available to the school's who used the original playing fields.

9. *The disposal of playing fields where they are not the school's only provision of playing fields but fall within section 77 only by reason of a school's temporary or occasional use of them. 'Temporary' meaning use as a school's main playing fields for a maximum of three school terms in the last 10 years or use only whilst the school's own playing fields could not be used by the school for reasons outside the school's or local authority's control.*
10. *The change of use of playing fields to allow the reconfiguration of school sites, where the following conditions are satisfied: (a) after the project is completed, the school will have at least the same size and quality of playing fields as it had before, with no net loss; (b) there is no disposal of playing fields; (c) the local authority and/or school ensures that the requirements of the School Premises Regulations 2012 continue to be met.*
11. *The change of use of playing fields to accommodate an expansion in pupil places at the same school site where the following requirements are met: (a) the loss of playing fields is a either 5% or less of the school's existing amount of playing fields regardless of whether the school will meet 100% of its guideline amount following the change of use or more than 5% but less than 15% of the school's existing amount of playing fields, where the school will continue to meet at least 100% of its guideline amount following a change of use; (b) in either case this paragraph 11 has not been relied on for another change of use of playing fields at the same school site within the past three years and provided also that the school supports the proposal.*

Even where general consent has been granted pursuant to the above Schedule, Para 5 of the general consent states that any consent is granted subject to the condition that the body seeking to dispose of or change the use of playing fields, is to comply with any relevant guidance published room time to time by the Secretary of State and also provide the Secretary of State with: (a) details of the location and area (in square metres) of the playing fields to be disposed of or have the use changed; (b) the area in square metres of the remaining playing field which is not subject to the disposal or change of use; (c) details of the total site area of the school in square metres; (d) the number of pupils on the school roll; (e) the date or proposed date of the disposal or change of use; (f) an explanation why the body considers that the disposal of the change of use is covered by a class consent; (g) a plan clearly identifying thearea in question in relation to the whole of the school sites; and (h) where the disposal or change of use is at an operating school, the views of the headteacher and governing body.

It will be seen from the above that where there is any proposal for the sale or change of use of playing fields as a working school, there are other parties to be involved, namely the head teacher and the governing body.

What this means, in practice, is that any proposal for the sale or change of use of active school playing fields requires the documented support of the headteacher and at least a majority of the school governors.

Open Space and Amenity Land

The constraints which affect the disposal or use of open space and other open-access amenity land depend on the particular legislation or trusts and which the land is held. At its most basic, section 164 of the Public Health Act 1875 (which is one of the 1875 Acts few surviving provisions) gives power to a local authority to lay out and maintain land for use of public walks or pleasure grounds and to contribute to the support of public walks or pleasure grounds provided by anyone. Section 164 also empowers local authorities to make bylaws for the management of those public walks and pleasure grounds.

But it is Section 10 of the Open Spaces Act 1906, which created the concept of a public trust, which applies to all public open space and burial grounds held by a local authority under that Act.

Section 10 provides that such land must be held and administered in trust to allow and with a view to enjoyment thereof by the public as public open space within the meaning of the Act and for no other purpose.

Other land within the ownership of the local authority may have the physical character of public open space, even though it is not held expressly either under the Acts of 1875 or 1906, but by some other local authority function, such as the housing revenue account, where it provides local amenity space connected with a housing development.

So long as there are no other legal constraints, land is held under the Acts of 1875 or 1906 may be sold or appropriated to other purposes provided that the advertisement requirements set out in section 123 (2) (A) of the Local Government Act 1972 are correctly followed and proper consideration given to any objections which are received.

Whilst the Section 123(2)(A) formalities are not administratively onerous, we have already seen, in the case of Day v Shropshire council, 2022, what can happen when those simple formalities are overlooked, which means that the statutory trust applying to the land is not overreached and therefore sterilising any alternative development potential. However, some public trusts cannot so easily be overreached.

The obvious example is registered common and town and village green, now subject to the Commons Act 2006. Another example is land which is held as 'green belt' under the Green Belt (London and Home Counties) Act 1938.

Note that statutory greenbelt held under the 1938 Act is not to be confused with the modern concept of greenbelt under town planning legislation, which has special policy-protections to prevent urban sprawl. Statutory greenbelt held under the 1938 Act predates modern town planning legislation, as introduced in 1947, and is more in the nature of public trust land.

Any sale or use of statutory greenbelt for other purposes requires Secretary of State consent under Sections 5 or 10 of the 1938 Act. And there is no general consent covering that.

Statutory greenbelt may often have been purchased long ago by several 'contributing authorities', which may have been the subject of abolition or amalgamation in successive local government reorganisations. Those other 'contributing authorities', to the extent that they still exist, will need to be formally notified of any proposal for the sale or change of use of that statutory greenbelt and may also have the right to veto such change.

You will know when you are dealing with statutory greenbelt, because there will usually be a restriction on the registered title (or unregistered title deeds) making express reference to the need to comply with 1938 Act formalities as regards any disposition of that land as well as other restrictive covenants designed to protect public access.

The main provision in the 1938 Act governing the disposal of statutory greenbelt by local authorities is Section 5, which requires any local authority proposing either to sell or appropriate to other purposes, statutory greenbelt which is within its ownership, to first of all publish in at least one local newspaper a notice of the proposal and specifying the time within which and the manner in which objections can be made and also serve a copy of such notice on every contributing local authority as well as on the relevant county council (if it still exists).

The local authority must also seek the consent of every contributing local authority and the county council to such sale, exchange or appropriation and also send to the minister a copy of any such notice and of every consent which has been obtained to such sale, exchange or appropriation obtained, when applying for the consent of the minister to the proposed sale or appropriation.

Before giving any such consent under Section 5, the minister is first required to consider any objections received to the proposed sale, exchange or appropriation and, if the consent of any contributing local authority or county council is not obtained by the local authority in whom the land is vested, the minister, before granting any consent, must first cause a local inquiry to be held.

Any ministerial order granting consent under Section 5 may contain such terms and conditions if any as shall appear to be just and, where such order is made with reference to the sale or appropriation of greenbelt, may also provide that the land to which the order relates shall be freed (to the extent specified) from the restrictions imposed on the land, whether by the 1938 Act or by any declaration made or covenant entered into in any manner provided and for the purposes of the 1938 Act.

As we have already seen, the statutory requirement to consult other contributing authorities as well as a county council might seem academic in circumstances where the local authority now owning the land is the statutory successor of any former county council as well as any other contributing authority.

That was certainly the case in *Regina v Secretary of State for the Environment, Transport and the Regions (Appellant) and others ex parte O'Byrne (respondent) [2003] 1 All ER 15*, when the House of Lords had to consider the interrelationship between the restrictions contained in the 1938 Act and the statutory right-to-buy under the Housing Act 1985.

In that case, the London Borough of Croydon, which owned the land, was the statutory successor to both the former Borough of Croydon as well as the former London County Council, who were the parties to a Deed dated 5 February, 1948, which concerned nine acres of land outside Croydon known as Coombe Wood, and which designated the land as statutory greenbelt for the purposes of the 1938 Act. Within the land was a stable block (now a café) above which was residential staff accommodation.

Miss O'Byrne was a landscape gardener employed by Croydon Council in that capacity since 1988. In 1993, the Council offered her a service tenancy of the Coombe Wood flat for the better performance of her duties as a gardener. She accepted the offer and, with her partner and the child moved into the flat. Their service tenancy was not a secure tenancy under the Housing Act 1985, which meant that she did not then have the statutory right-to-buy. However, in May 1994 the council engaged a private company, Serco, to take over the maintenance of Coombe Wood Park and her contract of employment was transferred by Croydon Council to Serco. That change in her employment status also meant that, technically, she was no longer a service tenant of Croydon Council, although she remained in occupation of the upstairs flat with her partner and her child.

The fact that she was no longer a service tenant of Croydon

Council meant that the status of their tenancy was converted, by operation of law, to that of a secure tenancy, carrying with it the statutory right-to-buy under the Housing Act 1985..

As the flat was within statutory greenbelt, Croydon Council advertised the proposed sale under the 1938 Green Belt Act and a public inquiry was held, following which the Secretary of State refused to give consent as required by Section 5 of the 1938 Act. The issue then was whether Miss O'Byrne's statutory right-to-buy overrode the restrictions on sale which would otherwise apply under the 1938 Act. The Lawlords held that Miss O'Byrne's right to buy prevailed.

In paragraph 31 of the judgment, Lord Bingham explained the background to the 1938 Act, which he said, provided for the manner in which a greenbelt around London would be established.

Either private owners or local authorities could declare their land to be greenbelt land and the enter into restrictive covenants for that purpose. In addition, local authorities were given power to purchase land for the purpose of it becoming greenbelt land or to contribute to the purchase price on the purchase of land for that purpose by some other local authority. Basic to the scheme was that the greenbelt land, whether privately owned or local authority owned, would be subject to suitable restrictive covenants. Section 10 of the Act also imposed restrictions on the erection of buildings on greenbelt Land.

In the 1948 Deed, whereby Coombe Wood became statutory greenbelt, the council, which had purchased the land for £14,000, entered into covenants with the former London County Council, which had contributed £2,732 to the purchase price. Those covenants were restrictive as to the use to which the land could be put. In particular there was a covenant, *"That the said lands or any part thereof shall not have any time hereafter be used without the written consent of the London Council previously had had obtained for any purpose other than a public open space within the meaning of the Open Spaces Act 1906 or for public walks and pleasure grounds or to provide for outdoor games or recreation. "*

There was a further covenant against any building on the land, other than a building which is ancillary to the authorised purposes for which the land or appropriate part thereof is for the time being used, unless the consent of the London Council shall have been first had and obtained.

Back in 1948, when the land was acquired, there was already at least one building on the land comprising stables and residential accommodation, it being easy to accept that both the café and Miss O'Byrne's occupation could be regarded as reasonably ancillary to the enjoyment of the park by the public and therefore consistent with the use restriction in the 1948 Deed.

Following the abolition of the former London County Council by the London Government Act 1963, the new London Borough of Croydon now became both the covenantor and the covenantee in respect of the restrictions contained in the 1948 Deed. But the status of the land as statutory greenbelt was not affected as, under section 23 of the 1938 Act, the restrictions remained enforceable by the minister.

In paragraph 44 of his judgment, Bingham was of the view that the Section 5 restrictions only applied when it was the local authority which was proposing sale, not when a sale was being forced on it by other legislation.

Note: in the O'Byrne case and in most other situations involving the sale or proposed change of use of statutory greenbelt land held under the 1938 Act, the land will also be subject to the express constraints of the Open Spaces Act 1906 or the Public Health Act 1875, which will in turn engage section 123(2A) of the 1972 Act, requiring statutory advertisement not just for a single week as specified in the 1938 Act but for two successive weeks, as required by the 1972 Act. In such circumstances, we would recommend that the statutory advertisement is drawn in a way which makes express reference to both the 1938 Act and also to the 1972 Act, so that it satisfies all statutory requirements affecting the sale or appropriation of that land.

Allotment Land

In the final part of this section, we look at allotment land, which is just as restrictive as any proposed sale of statutory greenbelt under the 1938 Act but arguably more difficult as allotment associations can be vociferous opponents of any proposal to sell allotment land or use it for other purposes.

The restriction on sale of allotment land is contained in Section 8 of the Allotments Act 1925, which states:

"Where a local authority has purchased or appropriated land for use as allotments, the local authority shall not sell, appropriate, use or dispose of land for any purpose other than used for allotments without the consent of the Minister of Agriculture and Fisheries and such consent may be given unconditionally or subject to such conditions as the minister thinks fit but shall not be given unless the minister is satisfied that adequate provision will be made for allotment holders displaced by the action of the local authority or that such provision is a necessary or not reasonably practicable."

It will therefore be seen that Section 8 of the 1925 Act imposes a presumption against the grant of consent for the sale of allotment land unless the local authority can prove that adequate alternative provision will be made for displaced allotment holders or that such revision is a necessary or not reasonably practicable.

Appropriation

Appropriation occurs when land originally acquired by a local authority for one statutory purpose, is no longer required for that original statutory purpose and its use can be better put to a different public use. Whilst it may be apparent from visible inspection that the land is no longer being used for its original purpose, formal appropriation from one statutory purpose to another statutory purpose has to be a documented process, involving a decision of cabinet or some other executive decision, followed by the execution of the document evidencing the fact that such appropriation has taken place and which will then form part of the title to the property.

It is also possible for there to be several successive appropriations of the same piece of land for different statutory purposes. When it comes to the law, our starting point has to be Section 122 of the Local Government Act 1972, which gives councils the general power to appropriate land owned by the local authority from one statutory function to another statutory function, without any legal change in the ownership of the property.

Section 122 (1) states: *"Subject of the following provisions of this section, a principle council may appropriate for any purpose for which the council are authorised by this or any other enactment to acquire land by agreement, any land which belongs to the council and is no longer required for the purpose for which it is held immediately before the appropriation; but the appropriation of land by a council by virtue of this section shall be subject to the rights of other persons in, over or in respect of the land concerned."*

Section 122 also contains similar constraints as would apply if the land is being sold pursuant to section 123 of the 1972 Act, particularly as regards open space, unless the proposed appropriation of that open space or other statutory purposes has previously been advertised for two successive weeks in the local press and due consideration given to any objections which have been received. It is also important to note, firstly that the power to an appropriate contained in section 122 only applies to 'principal' councils, namely districts, counties and unitaries, with towns and parishes having their own power of appropriation under section 120 of the 1972 Act.

The second issue is that appropriation to an alternative statutory use can only take place if it can be demonstrated that the use of the land for its original statutory purpose is no longer required. It is also important to have regard to any other statutory constraints affecting sale or use of land held for a particular statutory purpose (such as statutory greenbelt or allotments).

Neither do sections 122 and 126 of the Local Government Act 1972 exist in isolation, as there are also powers of appropriation contained in section 19 of the Housing Act 1985 as well as section 232 of the Town and Country Planning Act 1990, all of which are mutually exclusive. However all share the requirement to advertise any prospective appropriation of land comprising open space, so as to extinguish any public trust. We start with the relevant parts of section 19 of the Housing Act 1985, which is summarised below:

Section 19 Housing Act 1985 (Appropriation of Land)

A local housing authority may appropriate for the purposes of this Part any land for the time being vested in them or at their disposal; and the authority has the same powers in relation to land so appropriated as they have in relation to land acquired by them for the purposes of this Part.

(1) Where a local housing authority have acquired or appropriated land for the purposes of this Part, they shall not, without the consent of the Secretary of State, appropriate the whole or any part of the land consisting of a house or part of a house for any other purpose.

(2) The Secretary of state's consent may be given-

(a) either generally to all local housing authorities or to a particular authority or description of authority, and

(b) either in relation to particular land or in relation to land at a particular description;

and it may be given subject to conditions.

(3) The Secretary of state shall consult the Regulator of Social Housing before deciding whether to consent under this section to anything within the Regulator's remit.

Note: that the General Housing Consents referred to earlier in this chapter relate specifically to sales of HRA Land, not appropriations. However, the absence of such a general consent for appropriations is not problematic as the requirement for Secretary of State consent only applies where the land to be appropriated consists of a house or part of the house. Therefore there would seem to be no restriction on the appropriation of other HRA Land being appropriated to other purposes.

Section 232 of the Town and Country Planning Act 1990 contains the following power of the appropriation:

Section 232 – appropriation of land held for planning purposes

(1) Where any land has been acquired or appropriated by a local authority for planning purposes and is for the time being held by them for the purposes for which it was so acquired or appropriated, the authority may appropriate

the land for any purpose for which they are or may be authorised in any capacity to acquire land by virtue of or under any enactment not contained in this part or in Chapter V of Part I of the Planning Listed Buildings and Conservation Areas Act 1990.

The remainder of section 232 contains similar restrictions as regards common and open space..

Note. The only material difference between the specific powers of appropriation contained in section 19 of the Housing Act 1985 and section 232 of the Town and Country Planning Act 1990 is that, unlike section 1 to 2 of the Local Government Act 1972, a local authority is not first required to give specific consideration as to whether the land is still required for the purpose of which it was held immediately before the appropriation.

Where an appropriation takes place of land which is registered to a different statutory purpose, including obsolete legislation, such as the Housing Act 1957, it may be worthwhile updating any register of title to avoid issues in the future as regards the lawful use of the land and what constraints apply to it. As we will see in a later chapter, there may also be strategic reasons for appropriating land to the Town and Country Planning Act 1990, particularly where there is imminent redevelopment involved.

7 DRAFTING THE DOCUMENTATION

Even as this book is being written, the Law Society is consulting on a new "Code for Signing and Exchanging Property Contracts" to replace the exchange formulas 'A', 'B' and 'C', which have existed since the beginning of the 1980s.

Those three formulae were devised in the wake of changes in the way contracts were exchanged, which now had depended on a telephone conversation – or a series of telephone conversations – between conveyancers, accompanied by electronic monetary transfers, which enabled exchanges in back-to-back transactions to take place instantly instead of relying on the physical swapping of documentation and bankers' drafts, perhaps over the course of several days, which had been standard conveyancing practice hitherto.

Whilst those three formulae were noted for their simplicity, the same cannot be said for the Law Society's proposed replacement, which now runs to 14 pages of technical requirements. The backdrop to the latest changes is that, for many commercial transactions, the traditional wet-ink signature has given way to electronic signing platforms, such as Docusign, even if many local authority conveyancing teams are still catching up with these changes.

The second change is that conveyancing has now become a much more dangerous world than it was in the 1980s, where electronic fraud has never been easier, with fortunes at stake, and the chance of being caught, next to zero. No wonder professional Indemnity Insurers now see conveyancing as very high risk. But for in-house local authority conveyancers, there is something much more critical, which is why we have put it in bold.

Critical contract provisions governing the transmission and receipt of funds must be included in any contract for the purchase or sale of real estate between a council and another party to enable a smooth exchange of contracts or completion.

Once the new exchange protocol has been formally adopted, it will take its place with the Law Society's Code for Completion by Post 2019; the Standard Conditions of Sale, the Standard Commercial Property Conditions, the TA6 Property Information Form; and associated fixtures and fittings questionnaire, TA13 Completion Information and Undertakings Form as well as a raft of other TransAction forms, which govern the mainstream conveyancing process for the bulk of conveyancing transactions in England and Wales involving back-to-back exchanges and completions of residential chains.

They also work on the premise that funds, whether payable on exchange or on completion, will pass between regulated client accounts. But, without amendment, that standard documentation does not work for the type of in-house conveyancing transaction with which nd in-house corporate lawyer is more likely to be engaged, simply because they do not have access to a solicitor's client account.

Neither can we give another conveyancer professionally binding undertakings governing the transfer or receipt of monies, because we do not have direct control over money coming in and out of our organization.

We may have a good working relationship with members of the corporation's finance team but we don't have a finger on the button. We can't undertake to another party either to transmit funds or hold money to order.

In fact we might not even know that funds have been transmitted or received by our organization until we receive back that confirmatory e-mail from the council's finance team, which may be the following day after the previous day's transactions have been cashed up. Those are just the limitations within which we have to work.

In the next section, we look in more detail at the Standard Conditions of Sale (and Standard Commercial Conditions), focusing on those provisions which are most problematic to the transactions with which we have to deal.

The Standard Conditions of Sale (Fifth Edition – 2018 Revision)

The Standard Conditions of Sale are not stand alone but form the central two pages of a standard-form contract.

The fact that the Standard Conditions as well as all of the TA forms are copyright protected, means that an organisation which has not purchased the right to download and use those templates, cannot lawfully do so. It is also the standard contract used in the bulk of domestic residential conveyancing transactions.

But this copyright issue does not prevent the Standard Conditions being incorporated by cross-reference in other contract documentation. The most problematic standard conditions for local authority conveyancers without access to a solicitors' client account are firstly Standard Conditions 2.2.4 to 2.2.6 which relates to payment of contract deposits and which states:

2.2.4 The deposit is to be paid:

- *(a) By electronic means from an account held in the name of a conveyancer at a clearing bank to an account in the name of the seller's conveyancer or (in any case where condition 2.2.5 applies) a conveyancer nominated by him and maintained at a clearing bank or*
- *(b) To the seller's conveyancer or (in a case where a condition 2.2.5 applies) a conveyancer nominated by him by cheque drawn on a solicitor's or licensed conveyancer's client account.*

2.2.5 If before completion date the seller agrees to buy another property in England and Wales for his residence, he may use all or any part of the deposit as a deposit in that transaction to be held on terms to the same effect as this condition and condition 2.2.6.

2.2.6 Any deposit or part of the deposit not being used in accordance with condition 2.2.5 is to be held by the seller's conveyancer as stakeholder on terms that on completion it is paid to the seller with accrued interest.

Secondly, Standard Condition 6.7, which deals with payment of the completion monies and which states:

6.7 (means of payment)

The Buyer is to pay the money due on completion by a direct transfer of cleared funds from an account held in the name of a conveyancer at a clearing bank and, if appropriate, an unconditional release of a deposit held by a stakeholder'

If left unamended, these Standard Conditions would mean that the conveyancer on the other side of the transaction would be under no professional obligation to accept a payment – otherwise than by any direct funds-payment from a solicitor's client account – or – to pay a deposit or transfer completion funds from their own client account to another solicitor's client account.

In other words you would be relying on the goodwill of the other conveyancer to agree to a payment being received or paid otherwise than in accordance with the strict terms of the contract. We now turn to the Law Society's Code for Completion by Post 2019.

That code was revised in 2019 to further combat conveyancing-fraud by placing express responsibility on the seller's solicitor to ensure that the completion monies were not paid away to anyone except the person who was entitled to receive it. *That obligation is set out in paragraph 8 of the code in which the seller's solicitor undertakes:*

i. *To have the seller's authority to receive the purchase money on completion; and*
ii. *On completion to have the authority of the proprietor of each mortgage, charge or other financial incumbrance which were specified under*

paragraph 7 but has not then been redeemed or discharged, to receive the sum intended to repay it.

Like the Standard Conditions of Sale referred to above and the Standard Commercial Conditions, the Law Society Code for Completion by Post, throughout the document, presupposes that the balance of completion monies will pass from the client account of the buyer's lawyer to the client account of the seller's lawyer.

It follows, that an in-house solicitor without access to a client account, and who does not have direct control as regards either the transmission of funds of the treatment of funds received from another party, is never in a position to comply either with the Standard Conditions of Sale, as drawn, or the Law Society's Code for Completion by Post 2019, nor to give any undertaking to comply with any of those terms and conditions.

Therefore, unless the contract and protocol conditions are amended to allow for direct transfers to and from the main bank account of the local authority, the conveyancer acting for the other party is under no obligation to exchange or complete the transaction otherwise than by excepting or transferring funds for or to another solicitor's client account. For that reason it is critical that any conveyancing contract entered into between a local authority and another party which involves the transfer of funds, either on exchange or completion, contains the following suggested special conditions, or something to like effect.

Where property is being sold by the Council to another party.

"It is agreed that any contract deposit as well as the balance of the completion monies shall be paid from the client account of the Buyer's Conveyancer directly to the bank account of the Seller."

Where the property is being purchased by the Council from another party.

"It is agreed that any contract deposit shall be paid directly from the account of the

buyer to the client account of the seller's conveyancer [to be held by the seller's conveyancer as stakeholder pending completion of the transaction]. It is further agreed that the balance of the completion monies shall, on completion the transaction, be transmitted directly from the bank account of the buyer to the client account of the Seller's Conveyancer."

For the same reasons, where the council's conveyancer is asked to undertake to comply with the Law Society's Code for Completion by Post 2019, it is important that any undertaking given by the council's conveyancer to comply with the 2019 Code is qualified by the words, *"save as varied by the contract conditions regarding payment and receipt of funds"*.

Not having access to a solicitors client account and not having direct control over the transmission or receipt of funds also poses the following practical issues for the council's conveyancer, which need to be addressed either in the documentation or in the correspondence between lawyers in sufficient time before completion namely:

1. That the council's conveyancer can give no undertaking to transmit funds, because the mechanisms for the transmission or receipt of funds are not directly within the conveyancer's control but rely on cooperation from the council's finance team. The suggested solution is that arrangements are made for any contract deposit or completion monies to be transmitted across from the council's bank account to the client account of the receiving-conveyancer so that safe receipt of that money can be confirmed before the transaction exchanges or-as the case may be-the transaction completes. However any transmission of funds to a seller's conveyancer before the transaction exchanges are completes, has to be against the seller's conveyancer's written undertaking to hold that advance payment to your order until the transaction exchanges, or as the case may be, completes, when the monies can be released.
2. The council's solicitor can give no undertaking to hold any monies received, to the order of another party, because, again, those received funds are not within the conveyancer's direct

control. That is the position which the conveyancers for both parties have to accept.

The biggest practical issue is that there may be a delay on the part of the council's finance team in confirming receipt of funds, which may have reached the council's bank account several hours earlier.

What is important, before asking for a transmission of funds from another party, is that the council's conveyancer has everything they need, in terms of executed documentation (including authorisation to complete) to exchange or complete the transaction immediately, and on a telephone call, as soon as receipt of the money is has been confirmed.

If it is too problematic for the buyer's conveyancer to complete the transaction in this way, the alternative is for the buyer's conveyancer to provide written confirmation that they are holding funds for payment of the deposit-or as the case may be, the completion monies, and formerly undertake to transmit those funds by electronic transfer from their client account to the council's bank account, as soon as the relevant exchange or completion has taken place.

CPSEs – Commercial Property Standard Enquiries

Whilst use of the published Standard Conditions of Sale and related TransAction forms are restricted because of copyright protection, the same does not apply to the commercial property standard enquiries (published by the British Property Federation), which are freely downloadable and ask similar, but commercially more detailed, questions. Whilst the presumption is that the Standard Conditions and TA forms will be used for any residential transaction, for many commercial transaction, the CPSEs provide a viable alternative.

There is a range of CPSE templates, the most basic being the CPSE1, which covers all transactions, with supplemental CPSE templates for specific transactions, such as tenanted property or sale of reversions.

Statutory Authorisation for the Transaction

In any council sale or purchase of real estate, it is good conveyancing practice to state within the document the particular statutory power for which the land is being bought or sold.

This is important as it will help to avoid any Land Registry requisitions, when a sale is taken place but also to provide a reference point as regards any future dealings with the property.

For example, we will see in the next chapter, how lands purchased by a local authority specifically for planning purposes in connection with a proposed development for which planning permission has been obtained, will engage Section 203 of the Housing and Planning Act 2016, and convert any private third party rights which might otherwise impede the proposed development into a statutory right to compensation based on provable loss.

Where reliance is placed on a general consent (see above), to avoid the need to apply to the Secretary of State for express consent under any relevant legislation, it is also recommended, for the same reasons, that express reference to the general consent and the paragraphs relied on within that consent is set out in the transfer document or lease.

Ensuring the enforceability of covenants party (both positive and negative) against another party and their successors in title

In general, the enforceability of freehold restrictive covenants depends on the application of ancient rules of law and equity dating back to the landmark case of Tulk v Moxhay 1848. It means that the burden of a freehold restrictive covenant can only bind the successors in title of the original covenantor if it is negative in nature, touches and concerns the land, and is capable of benefiting other land belonging to the original covenantee or their successors in title.

In short, it is an imprecise science. Whilst positive covenants, such as obligation is to pay money, will not automatically bind successors in title of the original covenantor, there are other contractual devices which can be used to pass a payment obligation to successors in title of the original covenantor. This might include securing the payment by legal charge or imposing a restriction on the land registry title of the covenanting land, so that it cannot be leased or transferred unless the transferee has first entered into direct covenants with the benefitting party to make those payments.

Other ways of securing such payments might include an estate rent charge. Whilst, in most cases, obligations on a freehold owner to develop or use land in a particular way or pay money to another freehold owner (perhaps relating to the cost of maintaining communal facilities), for local authorities, there may be other economic or social reasons to impose covenants on freehold land which is being sold, even in circumstances where the local authority no longer owns or any neighbouring land which is capable of benefiting from those obligations.

Therefore specific mechanisms will need to be put in place, such as the entry of title restrictions or perhaps by putting in place the more cumbersome estate rent charge.

However, as will be seen in the next chapter, there may be easier ways in which a local authority can secure enforceability of freehold covenants, whether or not the council owns adjoining or neighbouring property, by utilising one of the several statutory mechanisms which provide for enforceability against successive owners.

However, such covenants will only be enforceable in that way if they are expressed to be made pursuant to those specific statutory provisions. Here is an example,

"It is agreed that the obligations on the part of the transferee set out in clauses 13.6 of this transfer are made pursuant to section 16 of the Greater London Council (General Powers) Act 1974 and enforceable by such against the transferee and its successors in title."

But it is not enough simply to make reference to the particular statute making the covenant enforceable against successors in title, that agreement, once completed, must then be registered as a local land charge against the property to ensure that anyone dealing with the property in the future is alerted to its existence.

Note that in this case, it is registration as a local land charge which triggers in its enforceability, not registration against the registered title.

The Court of Appeal judgment in Overseas Investment Services Ltd v Simcobuild Construction Limited and Swansea City Council, 1995, 70 P&CR 322 illustrates the importance of ensuring that statutory agreements made between the developer and the local authority, in that case relating to future the construction of a road, is binding on a successor in title, if the land on which the road is yet to be built is subsequently sold off. In that case, the Court of Appeal ruled that the Section 38 Highways Act 1980 road making agreement was not binding on that successor, which meant that the buyers of new houses on the estate were left without any right of access from their properties on to the nearest public highway.

The rationale of the judgment, as reported in The Independent, 27 March, 1995, is as follows:

"Rights created by an agreement made pursuant to section 38(3) Highways Act 1980 relation to the construction of a future highway over registered land, were not 'public rights' within the meaning of S70(1)(a) of the Land Registration Act 1925 [since superseded by the Land Registration Act 2002] and therefore not overriding rights binding on a subsequent purchaser of the land, since they were not rights exercisable by anyone merely by virtue of his being a member of the public and under general law."

The court also pointed out that the problem over enforceability against subsequent owners, would not have been arisen if the section 38 agreement had been expressed to be made pursuant to section 33 of the Local Government (Miscellaneous Provisions) Act 1982 and registered as a local land charge.

Is the contract binding on anyone?

Remember that any agreement which a local authority enters into with another party which involves the transfer of property must be sufficiently compliant with Section 2 of the Law of Property (Miscellaneous Provisions) Act 1989, which requires a land contract to be signed by both parties and contain all material terms, if it is to be enforceable through the courts.

The issue came to light in the case of Jelson Limited v Derby City council, 1999, when the High Court ruled invalid a clause in a planning agreements made pursuant to section 106 of the Town and Country Planning Act 1990 which, amongst other things, required the transfer of land by the developer to an unidentified housing association, on the grounds that the intended transferee of the affordable housing was not a signatory to the agreement. Justice Mackie said:

"A clause in an agreement under section 106 to the Town and Country Planning Act 1990 between the developer and the planning authority which obliged the developer to transfer an affordable housing site to a housing association to be nominated by the local authority was of no legal effect since there was no signature on behalf of the housing association as required by Section 2 of the Law of Property(Miscellaneous Provisions) Act 1989".

What is surprising is that the decision in Jelson has not triggered or any fundamental change in the way section 106 planning obligations are being drafted, which still include provisions obliging developers to transfer land to nominated housing associations who are not signatories to the agreement.

It just means that the section 106 agreement has to be drafted in a different way, so that it is no longer technically a contract for sale but instead an obligation on the developer not to allow occupation of a completed dwelling to take place until such a transfer has taken place.

An agreement structured in that way is not a contract for the sale of land, as the developer is not at that point under a legal obligation to transfer land to anyone. Instead, the developer is contracting not to allow occupation of a completed dwelling until conditions-precedent had been satisfied, namely the transfer of land to a housing association.

An agreement structured in that way is entirely within the ambit of section 106(1) of the Town and Country Planning Act 1990, which states:

> *(1) Any person interested in land in the area of a local planning authority may, by agreement or otherwise, enter into an obligation (referred to in this section and sections 106A and 106C as a "planning obligation") enforceable to the extent mentioned in subsection (3) –*
> *(a) restricting the development or use of the land in a specified way;*

(b) *requiring specified obligations or activities to be carried out in, on, under or over the land.*
(c) *requiring the land to be used in a specified way, or*
(d) *requiring a sum or sums to be paid to the local authority or, in the case where section 2E applies, to the Greater London Authority on a specified date or dates or periodically.*

Provided that a section 106 planning obligation conforms to any of these tests, it is likely to be valid and enforceable.

Registration formalities

We have already seen that for a section 38 highways agreement to be enforceable against a successor in title, it must be expressed to be made pursuant to section 33 of the Local Government (Miscellaneous Provisions) Act 1982, or another statutory provision to similar effect, and then registered as a local land charge.

Note that it is registration as a local land charge which is critical to the enforceability of a statutory agreements, not registration against the title to the property. Protection by registration at the Land Registry must however be considered when an agreement affecting a registered title is intended to bind successors in title of the original covenantor.

In the rarer case, where covenants are entered into affecting land for which there is no registered title, consideration should be given as to whether it should be registered under one of the categories of Land Charge now referred to in the Land Charges Act 1972 and disclosable on a K15 land such charges search.

Remember Part 25 of the Companies Act 2006, which requires any financial charge created by a registered company in the UK to be registered at Companies House within 21 days. This is in addition to any other registration requirement..

As the 21 day deadline is critical, it is recommended that the legal charge be uploaded electronically on to the Companies House website, which not only speeds up the process but also reduces the possibility of error. The risk with postal delivery is that by the time Companies House notifies you of a registration-error, you will already be out of time for registering the charge.

The only exception to the Companies House registration requirements are rent deposits paid to secure compliance with lease obligations. Note also that the requirement to register at Companies House might not only relate to the obvious charge by way of legal mortgage but may also extend to other agreements on the part of the company to pay money, which could take effect as if created by a legal charge.

The obvious example is section 7 of the Local Land Charges Act 1975 (the effect of registering certain financial charges), which states:

"A local land charge falling within Section 1(1)(a) above shall take effect as if it had been created by legal mortgage within the meaning of the Law of Property Act 1925 but without prejudice to the priority of the charge."

Section 1(1)(a) of the 1975 Act, refers to:

"Any charge acquired either before or after the commencement of the Act by a local authority or national park authority, water authority, sewerage undertaker, Public Health Acts 1936, 1937, 1961; Highways Act 1980; Building Act 1984, or similar charge acquired by a local authority or National Parks Authority under any other act, whether passed before or after this act, being a charge that is binding on successive owners of land affected."

Which means that any statutory agreement relating to the payment of money and which is registrable as a local land charge acts in the same way as if it is a financial charge under the Law of Property Act 1925, which are arguably means that it should be registered at Companies House and within 21 days of its creation.

Execution of documents by local authorities

A major cause of Land Registry requisitions concerns the execution of documents by local authorities. This includes whether the document has been executed in accordance with the required format prescribed by the council's own constitution.

Also whether the signatories-or single signatory-to that document, is someone authorised, within the terms of that constitution, to sign documents at that time on behalf of the local authority. One of the problems is that there is no single prescribed form of attestation clause for the execution of deeds by local authorities. And the problem is only likely to become more complex with the growth of electronic conveyancing, with which many local authorities are still catching up. When it comes to town and parish councils, the issue is more clearly addressed in Section 14(3) of the Local Government Act 1972, which states:

"Notwithstanding anything in any rule of law, a parish council need not have a common seal but where a parish council have no seal, any act of theirs which is required to be signified by an instrument under seal may now be signified by an instrument signed and sealed by two members of its council."

For counties, districts and unitaries, the process for attesting any deed is whatever is contained in the council's adopted constitution for the time being. But as we have already seen, a local authority constitution is not usually drafted with the legal precision of a conveyancing document or a company's articles of association. So it is all about interpretation.

Our starting point therefore has to be Land Registry Practice Guide No 8, Execution of Deeds, and in particular Section 7 of that document, 'Execution of Deeds by Local Authorities'. The key part of that advice reads:

"In addition to the default forms of execution set out in Execution of Deeds By Other Corporations incorporated in the UK, many local authorities delegate authority to execute deeds and documents to various senior officers. Principal councils can avoid having to produce evidence each time by emailing it to us at localauthorityexecution@landregistry.gov.uk, so we can record it centrally. When executing deeds, the name or office of the signatories as appropriate should be included so we can be sure it is correctly executed." Where an alternative form of execution is used, and so long as it is in accordance with the council's adopted constitution, the application for registration should include the following certificate issued by an individual conveyancer employed by the relevant local authority and stating that the deed has been duly and properly executed in accordance with the councils constitution.

The recommended wording for such a certificate is as follows: "*I [name of conveyancer] a conveyancer employed by {name of authority] certify that the transfer [or other deed submitted for registration] dated [date of deed] is made by the authority of the council and has been duly and properly executed in accordance with the council's constitution.*"

Whilst we have only dealt with deeds and documentation executed by the local authority, a conveyancer acting for a local authority in a transaction involving another corporate entity, will need to ensure that the document is properly executed by both parties.

Special precautions need to be taken when the company on the other end of the transaction is registered in another jurisdiction (which includes companies registered in the Channel Islands, Isle of Man and other dependencies), when it is important to be able to evidence that the document was correctly executed in accordance with the laws of that other jurisdiction.

As a matter of course, this will involve obtaining formal certification from a qualified lawyer practising in that jurisdiction, that the off-shore company is entitled to enter into the transaction and that the documentation was properly executed in accordance with the laws of that jurisdiction.

To help combat property fraud, off-shore companies owning, or intending to purchase, property within the UK are now required to join the Register of Overseas Entities and also register at Companies House. For more information on dealing with off-shore companies, reference should be made to Land Registry Practice Guide 78 "Overseas Companies and LLPs". We would also recommend that when dealing with an offshore company, these specific conveyancing issues are addressed between solicitors before contracts are exchanged, to ensure that getting certification of due execution of the documentation from a lawyer practising in the particular jurisdiction does not become a last minute conveyancing issue.

Preparing a property for auction sale or sale by sealed tender

Preparing a property for auction sale requires a special skill as, once documentation is a loaded on to the auction website, there is no opportunity for negotiation as there would be one of sale by private treaty. If prospective bidders don't like what is being offered, or the way that it is being offered, they simply will not bid.

Therefore, it is important that the documentation uploaded contains everything which the buyer's conveyance will need to complete the transaction and that, critically, the terms of sale do not contain anything of an unnecessarily onerous nature likely to deter a prospective bidder or reduce the amount of the bids.

A typical auction pack will include: up to date copies of the title; standard conveyancing searches; replies to standard pre-contract enquiries; special conditions of sale; energy performance certificate; a draft of the transfer or other disposition which the successful purchaser will be required to enter into; and the special conditions of sale. It is of course important that the special conditions of sale address in detail the manner in which monies are to be received, in the absence of a solicitors client account (see above).

Once the auction is taken place, and assuming that the property has been sold above its reserve, the transaction can be brought straight to completion.

A similar approach is required where, as is sometimes the case, a property is being sold by sealed tender, where prospective purchasers submit their bids in secrecy and on paper, each with a deposit cheque equating to 10% of their bid, which will only be cashed if the bid is successful. A sale by sealed tender is also to be contrasted with a sale by "informal tender', in which nothing is binding until an exchange of contracts actually takes place.

8 LEGAL RESOURCES

In this chapter, we look at some of the specific legal resources which are available to local councils to overcome conveyancing issues which would otherwise become problematic, particularly when it comes to the acquisition, sale or appropriation of land for redevelopment.

Some of the statutory powers have already been touched on in earlier chapters but we now look at them again in greater detail as well as some additional statutory powers.

Overreaching Third Party Rights

To facilitate the carrying out of development for which planning permission has been obtained, the following statutory provisions enable local authorities to overreach certain private third-party rights which might otherwise impede the carrying out of the proposed redevelopment. It achieves this by converting any rights which the third party might otherwise have to injunct the carrying out of the development, into a statutory right to compensation. We start with Section 203 of the Housing and Planning Act Act 2016, which replaced the earlier legislation, to similar effect, contained in Section 237 of the Town and Country Planning Act 1990, and which now reads as follows:

"203 Power to override easements and other rights

(1) A person [which may mean either the local authority or its successor in title] may carry out building or maintenance work to which this subsection applies even if it involves-
   (a) interfering with a relevant right or interest, or
   (b) overreaching a restriction as to the use of land arising by virtue of a contract.
(2) Subsection (1) applies to building or maintenance work where-
   (a) There is planning consent for the building or maintenance work,
   (b) The work is carried out on land that has at any time on or after the date on which this section comes into force –
      (i) become vested in or acquired by a specified authority [see below],or
      (ii) been appropriated by a local authority for planning purposes as defined by Section 246(1) of the Town and Country Planning Act 1990.
   (c) The authority could acquire any land compulsorily for the purposes of the building or maintenance work, and
   (d) The building or maintenance work is for purposes related to the purposes for which the land was vested acquired or appropriated as mentioned in paragraph (b).
(3) [extends the power of overreaching third party rights where the building of maintenance work is to be carried out on other qualifying land].
(4) - 6 [extends the overreaching to uses of land as opposed to physical development or works.]

Notes . When section 203 is used to overreach private third party rights, that overreaching will benefit not only the local authority which acquired or appropriated land for planning purposes but also any successor in title who will be carrying out the actual development or works or change of use for which planning permission has been obtained. However, it is important that the overreaching actually occurs whilst the land is within the ownership of the local authority, both on the date the relevant planning permission granted and also when the appropriation takes place.

It must also be assumed (for the purposes of subsection (2)(d)), that had the land not already been within the council's ownership, the local authority would have been entitled to use compulsory purchase powers to acquire it.

It also follows that the overreaching powers provided by section 203 can only be exercised by a local authority which has both compulsory purchase powers and statutory town planning functions, which means that a parish or town council could not take the benefit of such overreaching unless as a successor in title to the county, district or unitary which owned the land at the time the planning permission was granted and when the appropriation (where applicable) took place.

Exclusions. There are some third party rights which cannot be overreached by appropriation under section 203, namely:
- Public rights of way [Section 203 (9)(a)]
- Rights or interests belonging to the National Trust [Section 203 10)]
- Rights belonging to public utilities and telecommunications operators, which are defined as 'Protected Rights [Section 205(1)] but which can be overreached by use of other legislation, see below.
- Occupational interests, which cannot be 'relevant interests' for the purposes of Section 203(1). A 'relevant interest' is defined as any easements, liberty, privilege, right or advantage annexed or to land and adversely affecting other land (including any natural right of support).

Process Before section 203 can be engaged, the land must have been acquired or appropriated for planning purposes. However land can only be acquired or appropriated for planning purposes if it is acquired or appropriated for one of the reasons set out in section 2 to 6 of the Town and Country Planning Act 1990.

In other words, the local authority have to make a policy decision that the land has to be acquired or appropriated for a specific development or for planning purposes. The first stage is therefore to obtain an executive resolution or decision as to why the land has to be purchased or appropriated for that specific purpose.

The appropriation itself then has to be documented for the record, perhaps in the form of a written memorandum signed on behalf of the local authority and defining the land and the development purpose for which it has been acquired or appropriated, making reference to the relevant planning permission authorising that development or change of use.

Like compulsory purchase, an appropriation or overreaching of third party rights engages the European Convention on Human Rights, as brought into domestic law by the Human Rights Act 1998, which is another issue which has to be addressed.

In that respect, it is important to try to identify any third party rights which are known to be affected and, where it is possible to do so, negotiate a release.

Compensation for Overreaching

This is dealt with in section 204 of the Housing and Planning Act 2016, which are set out below: 204 Compensation for overridden easements etc

(1) A person is liable to pay compensation for any interference with a relevant right or interest or breach of a restriction as is authorised by section 203.
(2) The compensation is to be calculated on the same basis as compensation payable under sections 7 and 10 of the Compulsory Purchase Act 1965.
(3) Where a person other than a specified or qualifying authority is liable to pay compensation under this section but has not paid-
   (a) the liability is enforceable against the authority, but
   (b) the authority may recover from that person any amount it pays out.
(4) The specified or qualifying authority against which a liability is enforceable by virtue of subsection (3)(a) is a specified or

qualifying authority in which the land to which the compensation relates is vested, or by which the land was acquired or appropriated as mentioned in section 203.
(5) Any dispute about compensation payable under this section may be referred to and determined by the Upper Tribunal.

Overreaching public utility and telecommunications rights

The extinguishment of public utility and telecommunications rights is specifically excluded from the overreaching provisions contained in section 203 of the Housing and Planning Act 2016 but is provided for in Part XI of the Town and Country Planning Act 1990, headed Extinguishment of Rights of Statutory Undertakers, etc. Here are the relevant sections (summarised):

Section 271 deals with the situation where land has been acquired or appropriated by a local authority for planning purposes and there exists within the land rights or apparatus belonging to a statutory undertaker for the purposes of the carrying out their function and the council are satisfied that the extinguishment of that right or the removal of apparatus is necessary for the purpose of carrying out any development with a view to which the land was acquired or appropriated.

In that event, the council can serve notice on the statutory undertakers stating that at the event of the prescribed period, the right will be extinguished or requiring that before the end of that period, the apparatus must be removed.

The recipient of that notice then has 28 days to serve a counternotice saying that they object to all or any of the provisions of the notice and specifying the grounds of their objection. In the absence of a counternotice, the right is extinguished at the end of the initial notice. And any apparatus must be removed.

However, if a counter notice is served, the local authority can either withdraw its initial notice (without prejudice to its ability to serve a further notice) or alternatively apply to the Secretary of State for an order confirming the notice with or without modification. Section 272 of the Act contains similar provisions in relation to rights and equipment belonging to telecommunications code system operators. Section 273 contains reverse provisions entitling a statutory undertaker to serve notice of entry on a local authority in circumstances where land has been acquired or appropriated for planning purposes and the statutory undertaker needs to get on to the land to remove or recycle apparatus or such part of if it is specified in the notice.

Again, the local authority receiving notice, has 28 days to object, in which case it is for the statutory undertaker to either withdraw their notice or apply to the Secretary of state for confirmation of that notice with or without modification.

Overreaching Occupancy Rights

Not all third party rights which might get in the way of a proposed redevelopment will be shown on the register of the land-title. An example of such an overriding right might be the prescriptive right of way acquired by the owner of adjoining property through long-user and which is currently in actual use.

However, chief amongst these are overriding rights, are the rights of persons in actual occupation of land including, notably, the rights of local authority secure tenants. Most local authority secure tenancies under the Housing Act 1985 are not drafted with the precision of a private sector residential tenancy.

In fact, the tenancy agreement may be nothing more than a two page pro-forma containing a photograph of the tenant, the fortnightly rent, and their signature, and making cross-reference to a brochure setting out the counci'ls standard terms and conditions.

Don't expect to find a plan showing the extent of the land comprised in the tenancy. Nor any express reservations giving the council and any development partner the right to come on to the tenanted-property, where necessary to facilitate the carrying out of a development on adjoining land.

All this makes it difficult for the local authority or its development partner to carry out works which may affect a secure tenant's enjoyment of their property. Everything may then depend on the tenant's willingness to cooperate with the council or its development partner, perhaps in return for some financial advantage. But where a tenant refuses to cooperate, what can the council or its development partner do?

Grounds 10 and 10A of Schedule 2 of the Housing Act 1985 allows a local authority, in certain circumstances, to obtain possession from a secure tenant where the dwelling itself is required for demolition and redevelopment.

But often, there is no proposal for demolition. All that the council or its development partner want to do is to re-align the boundaries of the property to fit in with the neighbouring redevelopment. Or perhaps to build on to the wall of the property or, maybe, erect scaffolding. For those reasons, our view is that the tenant should be included in any party wall notices or correspondence, even if only as a matter of courtesy.

As will be seen later in this chapter, the Party Wall etc Act may provide a solution if the tenant is engaged in the process. As we have seen, the powers contained in section 203 Housing and Planning Act 2016 does not extend to the extinguishment of occupancy rights.

However, the following powers can assist in bringing an end to a short term or periodic tenancy which might otherwise impede redevelopment, where land has been acquired or appropriated for planning purposes.

Section 242 of the Town and Country Planning Act 1990 (overriding of rights of possession), which enables the Secretary of State to certify that possession of a house which has been acquired or appropriated by a local authority for planning purposes and is immediately required for the purposes for which it was acquired or appropriated, in which case the local authority is empowered to obtain possession of the house notwithstanding anything in the Rent Act 1977 or Part 1 of the Housing Act 1988 (assured tenancies) which would otherwise prevent possession being obtained. Grounds 10 and 10A of Schedule 2 to the Housing Act 1985 (statutory grounds for possession), enables a local authority to obtain possession of a dwelling let under a secure tenancy where the property is required for redevelopment within a reasonable time.

Note that Ground 10 only applies to demolition and redevelopment which the local authority intends to carry out itself. The wider ground 10A provides a ground for possession when the local authority is intending to sell off the dwelling is part of scheme of development which has been approved by the Secretary of State
 .Compulsory purchase – see the next chapter.

Extinguishment of Public Rights

Here, we are talking about public rights of way for which there are powers of the extinguishment contained in section 116 the Highways Act 1980 as well as Part X of the Town and Country Planning Act 1990.

Statutory tools to ensure the enforceability of restrictive and positive covenants against successors in title.

We have seen from the case of Overseas Investment Services Ltd v Simcobuild Construction Ltd and Swansea City Council 1995, how the failure to use powers contained in section 33 of the Local Government (Miscellaneous Provisions) Act 1982 meant that a section 38 highways agreement was unenforceable against a successor in title to the original developer who entered into that agreement.

The failure of that section 38 agreement meant that the owners of new-build properties who had placed reliance on it to secure the adoption of roadways on the estate, were effectively land locked. Had the matter not been resolved between Swansea City council and that successor in title, the only alternative means of accessing the estate from the nearest public highway would have been to demolish two of the houses and to bulldoze a way through. Fortunately, such drastic action was not necessary but it became a powerful negotiating tool between the two parties,

The purpose of the several statutory tools outlined in this section is to provide a means of overcoming the common law and equitable constraints which would otherwise limit the enforceability of such covenants against successors in title.

Under the principles outlined in Tulk v Moxhay, 1848, the enforceability of a covenant against a successor in title of the original covenant or depended on it being negative in nature and the vendor retaining neighbouring property which was capable of being benefited by that covenant.

However many covenants signed by landowners in favour of a local authority are designed to secure a wider public benefits which are not intended to provide any benefit directly to neighbouring land. As such, those covenants, which predominantly will involve the payment of money or carrying out of works, would not, in the ordinary course of events, be binding on the successors in title of the original covenantor. This is the purpose of the following statutory provisions to redress that unsatisfactory common law situation. Here they are (in chronological order).

Section 16 Greater London Council (General Powers) Act 1974 (undertaking and agreements binding successive owners).

(1) Every undertaking given to a local authority by the owner of any legal estate in land and every agreement made between local authority and any such owner being an undertaking or agreement –
 (a) given or made under seal in connection with the land; and
 (b) expressed a to be given or made in pursuance of this section,
Shall be enforceable not only against the owner joining in the undertaking or agreement but also against the successors in title of any owner so joining and any person claiming through or under them.

(2) Such an undertaking or agreement shall be treated as a local land charge for the purposes of the [Local Land Charges Act 1975].
(3) Any person against whom such an undertaking or agreement is enforceable, shall be entitled to require a copy thereof from the local authority without payment.
(4) Any charge on the land which by virtue of this section is enforceable in the manner described in section (1) shall, for the purposes of subsection (1) of section 32 of the Building Societies Act 1962 (which prohibits advances by building societies on second mortgage), be deemed and not to be a prior mortgage within the meaning of that section.
(5) [Deals with repeals of earlier enactments]
(6) Any undertaking or agreement which by virtue of an enactment included in Part III of Schedule 2 or Part III of Schedule 3 to this Act was, immediately before the passing of this Act, binding on any successors in title of any owner joining in such undertaking or agreement and on any person claiming through or under them shall, notwithstanding, the repeal of that enactment, continue to be so binding and enforceable as if such undertaking or agreement were expressed to be given or made in pursuance of this section.
(7) In this section "local authority" means the Council or a borough council.

Notes to Section 16.

This is a local enactment which can only be used by London Boroughs to enter into undertakings or agreements which bind successors in title.

The use of the words, 'undertaking' and 'agreement', in place of 'covenant' suggest that it also relates to the enforceability of positive covenants against successors in title, including obligations relating to the payment of money.

Critical to the enforceability of a section 16 undertaking or agreement is firstly that it is executed as a Deed within the meaning of

Section 1 of the Law of Property (Miscellaneous Provisions) Act 1989. Secondly to its registration as a local land charge against the property which, in the case of a financial obligation, would take effect as a charge by way of legal mortgage against the land and which is capable of being converted into a charge against the registered title.

Where it is a registered UK Company which is entering into the financial obligation, remember the need to register the agreement, concurrently, at Companies House within the critical 21 day window for doing this.

Section 33 Local Government (Miscellaneous Provisions) Act 1982 (enforceability by local authorities of certain covenants relating to land).

(1) The provisions of this section shall apply if a principal council (in the exercise of their powers under Section 111 of the Local Government Act 1972 or otherwise) and any other person are parties to an instrument under seal which –
   (a) is executed for the purpose of securing the carrying out of works on land in the council's area in which the other person has an interest, or
   (b) is executed for the purpose of regulating the use of or is otherwise connected with land in or outside the council's area in which the other person has an interest.

and which is neither executed for the purpose of facilitating nor connected with the development of the land in question.

(2) If, in a case where this section applies,,-
   (a) The instrument contains a covenant on the part of any person having an interest in the land, being a covenant to carry out works or do any other thing on or in relation to that land, and
   (b) The instrument defines the land to which the covenant relates, being land in which that person has an interest at the time the instrument is executed, and

(c) The covenant is expressed to to be one to which this section or section 1 to 6 of the Housing Act 1974 (which is superseded by this section) applies,

The covenant shall be enforceable (without any limit of time) against any person deriving title from the original covenantor in respect of his interest in any of the land defined as is mentioned in paragraph (b) above and any person deriving title under him in respect of any lesser interest as if that person had also been an original covenanting party in respect of the interest for the time being held by him.

(3) Without prejudice to any other method of enforcement of a covenant falling within subsection (2) above, if there is a breach of the covenant in relation to any of the land to which the covenant relates, then subject to subsection (4) below, the principal councils who are a party to the instrument in which the covenant is contained that may –
   (a) enter on the land concerned and carry out the works or do anything which the covenant requires to be carried out or done or remedy anything which has been done and which the covenant required not to be done; and
   (b) recover from any person against whom the covenant is enforceable (whether by virtue of subsection (2) above or otherwise) any expenses incurred by the council in exercise of their powers under this subsection.

(4) Before a principal council exercise their powers under subsection (3)(a) above they shall give not less than 21 days notice of their intention to do so to any person-
   (a) who has for the time being an interest in the land or in relation to which the works are to be carried out or other thing is to be done; and
   (b) against whom the covenant is enforceable (whether by virtue of subsection (2) above or otherwise).

(5) If a person against whom a covenant is enforceable by virtue of subsection (2) above requests, the principal council shall supply him with a copy of the covenant, and it shall be their duty to do so free of charge.

(6) The Public Health Act 1936 shall have effect as if any reference in that Act in –
  (a) Section 283 of that Act (notices to be in writing; forms of notices, etc.),
  (b) Section 288 of that Act (penalty for obstructing execution of Act), and
  (c) Section 291 of that Act (certain expenses recoverable from owners to be a charge on the premises, or power to order payment by instalments),
included a reference to subsections (1) to (4) above and as if for any reference in those sections of that Act: (i) to a local authority where reference to a principal council; and (ii) to the owner of the premises where a reference to the holder of an interest in the land.

(7) – (10) [contain other supplemental provisions relating to the interpretation of this legislation, which is not repeated at length].

Notes to Section 33.

Although for London Boroughs, the section 33 power runs concurrently with the section 16 power, referred to above, its use is, in our opinion, much narrower than the section 16 power in its use of the word 'covenant' instead of 'agreement' or 'undertaking'.

The power conferred by section 33, which has been rolled out to all local authorities in England and Wales, is primarily related to the carrying out obligations relating to the carrying out of works on the affected land or in restricting the use or development of that land. There is no mention of section 33 covering a landowner's monetary obligations, save as regards the recovery of costs for default works.

Although section 33 makes no express reference to registration of its covenants as local land charges, the need for such registration is implicit in the Local Land Charges Act 1975.

As has already been seen from the case of Overseas Investment Services Ltd. V Simcobuild Construction Ltd and Swansea City

Council, 1995 70 PandCR 322, express reference to enforceability under section 33 is critical to a section 38 highways agreement [and any other statutory agreement of a similar nature] and registration of that agreement is a local land charge, is critical, if it is to be enforceable against successors in title of the original developer, as such statutory agreements are not deemed to be in the nature of 'public rights' and are not therefore an overriding interest for the purposes of land registration.

Section 609 Housing Act 1985 (enforcement of covenants against owner for the time being)

Where-
  (a) A local housing authority have disposed of land held by them for any of the purposes of this Act and/or the person to whom the disposal was made has entered into a covenant with the local authority concerning the land, or
  (b) An owner of any land has entered into a covenant with the local housing authority concerning the land to the purposes of any of the provisions of this Act,

The authority may enforce the covenant against the persons deriving title under the covenantor, notwithstanding that the authority are not in possession of or interested in any land for the benefit of which the covenant was entered into, in like manner and to the like extent as if they had been possessed of or interested in such land.

Notes to Section 609. It is apparent from the Supreme Court decision in Michael Cantrell v Wycombe District Council, [2008] EWCA Civ 866, that this is the most limited of the statutory powers referred to in this section. It is limited because in the Cantrell case, the Supreme Court ruled that section 609 could only apply to negative covenants and not anything of a positive nature, such as offering the local authority the right to nominate occupants of affordable housing, even though that local authority had paid money to Warden HousingAssociation, which had entered into the original covenant.

Section 106 Town and Country Planning Act 1990 (Planning Obligations)

(1) Any person interested in land in the area of a local planning authority may, by agreement or otherwise, enter into an obligation (referred to in this section and sections 106A to 106C and Schedule 7A as "a planning obligation"), enforceable to the extent mentioned in subsection (3)-
   (a) Restricting the development or use of land in any specified way;
   (b) Requiring specified operations or activities to be carried out in, on, under or over the land;
   (c) Requiring the land to be used in any specified way; or
   (d) Requiring a sum or sums to be paid to the authority (or, in a case where section 2E applies, to the Greater London Authority) on a specified date or dates or periodically.

In the case of a 'development consent obligation', by reference to development in (1A), subsection (1)(a) includes anything that constitutes development for the purposes of the Planning Act 2008

(2) A planning obligation may-
   (a) Be conditional or subject to conditions;
   (b) Impose any restriction or requirement mentioned in subsection (1)(a) to (c) either indefinitely or for such period or periods as may be specified and;
   (c) If it requires a sum or sums to be paid, require the payment of a specified amount or an amount determined in accordance with the instrument by which the obligation is entered into and, if it requires the payment of periodicals sums, require them to be paid indefinitely or for a specified period.

(3) Subject to subsection (4) a planning obligation is enforceable by the authority identified in accordance with subsection (9)(d)-
   (a) against that person entering into the obligation; and
   (b) against any person deriving title from that person.

(4) The instrument by which a planning obligation is entered into may provide that a person shall not be bound by the obligation in respect of any period during which he no longer has an interest in the land.

(5) The restriction or requirement imposed under a planning obligation is enforceable by injunction.

(6) Without prejudice to subsection (5), if there is a breach of any requirement in a planning obligation to carry out any operations in, on, under or over the land to which the obligation relates, the authority by whom the obligation is enforceable may –
   (a) enter the land and carry out the operations; and
   (b) recover from the person or persons against whom that the obligation is enforceable any expenses reasonably incurred by them in doing so.

(7) Before an authority exercise their power under subsection (6)(a), they shall give not less than 21 days notice of their intention to do so to any person against whom the planning obligation is enforceable.

(8) Any person who wilfully obstructs a person acting in the exercise of a power under subsection (6)(a) shall be guilty of an offence and liable on summary conviction to a fine not exceeding level three on the standard scale.

(9) A planning obligation may not be entered into except by an instrument executed as a deed which-
   (a) states that the obligation is a planning obligation for the purposes of this section and if the obligation is a development consent obligation, contains a statement to that effect.
   (b) identifies the land in which the person entering into the obligation is interested;
   (c) identifies the person entering into the obligation and states what his interest in the land is; and
   (d) identifies the local planning authority by whom that the obligation is enforceable and, if in a case where section 2E

applies, identifies the Mayor of London as an authority by whom the obligation is also enforceable.

(10) A copy of any such instrument shall be given to the authority so identified, the local planning authority so identified and, in the case with section 2E applies, to the Mayor of London.

(11) A planning obligation shall be a local land charge and for the purposes of the Local Land Charges Act 1975 the authority by whom the obligation is enforceable shall be treated as the originating authority as regards such a charge.

(12) Regulations may provide for the charging on the land of-
   (a) any sum or sums required to be paid under a planning obligation; and
   (b) any expenses recoverable by a local planning authority or the Mayor of London under subsection (6)(b), and of this section and sections 106A to 106BC shall have affect subject to any such regulations.

(13) In this section "specified" means a specified in the instruments by which the planning obligation is entered into and in this section and section 106A "land" has the same meaning as in the Local Land Charges Act 1975. In this section and section 106A "development consent obligation" means a planning obligation entered into in connection with the an application (or a proposed application) for an order granting development consent.

Enforcing restrictive covenants – Additional Tools

We have already mentioned the landmark decision in Tulk v Moxhay 1846, which laid down the rules of equity which enabled the burden of negative covenants, which touched and concerned the land, to be passed down to successors in title of the original covenantor in circumstances where the original covenantee (for whose benefit the covenant was expressed to be made), or their successors in title, retained adjoining or neighbouring land which was capable of enjoying the benefits from the restrictive covenant..

However, even when the local authority transferring land does not retain adjoining or neighbouring land capable of benefiting from a covenant, there are other conveyancing tools which can fill the gap. Here are some examples.

1. A clause in a transfer which requires any purchaser of the land to first enter into a direct deed of covenant with the local authority to observe and perform the relevant covenants, whether positive or negative. A restriction would then need to be registered on the title to prevent any future purchaser from registering their title unless the purchaser had first entered into the required deed of covenant with the original vendor.
2. The Contracts (Rights of Third Parties) Act 1999, which enables the parties to an agreement to specify that a particular covenant is expressed to be for the benefit of a third party, who will then have the right to enforce that provision directly in a court of law, even though they were not party to the original contract.
3. An estate rent charge – which is a survivor from the general abolition of new rent charges by the Rents Charges Act 1977, and which enables the charge to recover specified estate service charges from freeholders having use of those services.

The Ministry of Housing and Local Government Provisional Order Confirmation (Greater London Parks and Open Spaces) Act 1967.

This little known piece of local legislation gives London Boroughs express statutory power to carry out certain works and uses on public open space (including in some circumstances common land and town and village greens), which would otherwise have to remain undeveloped and open at all times to public access. This also includes disused burial grounds for which local authorities have taken over ownership or other management responsibility under the Open Spaces Act 1906. These express powers are summarised below:

As regards open space, Section 7 allows London Boroughs tomaintain: swimming and bathing facilities; golf courses and other open air facilities; gymnasium; rifle ranges; indoor recreation facilities; centres and other facilities for the use of clubs, societies and other organisations wholly or mainly of a recreational, social or educational character; providing amusement fairs and entertainments; outdoor ice skating facilities in times of frost; sale of meals and refreshments; provision of swings and associated children's facilities; provision of park-keeper accommodation. There are also provisos, namely that: free public access is not precluded at times when those facilities are not being used; any part of an open space set apart for enclosed four entertainment must not exceed one acre or one-10th of the open space; whichever is the greater. There are however restrictions on the showing of films on a commercial basis.

Section 8 allows London Boroughs, on such financial terms as they deem appropriate, to lease or licence to third parties the powers referred to in Section 7 above, which may also include the ability of the local authority to contribute towards or guarantee the expenses incurred by such third party in the provision of any entertainments or otherwise in pursuance of such grants or letting.

Section 9 enables councils to enclose any part of an open space for the purpose of the cultivation or preservation of vegetation in the interests of public amenity or in the interests of the safety of the public.

Section 10 enables councils to make reasonable charges for the use of facilities so provided.

Section 11 makes clear that the powers contained in the 1967 legislation override any other legislative restrictions but still take subject to other third party rights..

Section 12 relates specifically to common land (which will include registered town and village green) and prohibits the erection of any building or other structure or permanent enclosure except with the consent of the appropriate minister, who may also cause a local inquiry to be held before granting such consent.

Section 13 allows a local authority, either alone or in cooperation with another association or body, to organise or conduct any competition, including the setting apart an open space for this purpose to a maximum of one acre or one 10th of the open space, whichever is the greater. Again, the local authority may charge entrance fees to competitors as well as anyone else attending.

Section 14 enables to local authorities to reach agreement with each other as regards the management of any open space.

Section 15 states that for the purpose of enlarging or improving any open space, a local authority may enter into an agreement with the owner of adjacent land for exchanging land for open space and for associated financial adjustments between the parties.

Section 16 confers power on anyone owning land other than a local authority to enter into an agreement with the local authority to grant to that local authority the right of pre-emption to the local authority giving it a right of first refusal on any future sale, for the purpose of providing open space or for any other purpose under the Physical Training and Recreation Act 1937 at an agreed price.

Section 17 allows a local authority to exchange or other land for public open space.

Section 18 allows a local authority to appoint a parks-constabulary to patrol its open spaces but without the same powers of arrest as the mainstream constabulary except when in uniform and provided with a warrant.

Section 19 allows any parks-constable to enforce bye laws relating to an open space and to arrest anyone committing or have been committed any offence against such bylaws, whose name or residents is unknown to and cannot be ascertained by such officer or constable. The arrested person must then be taken to the police station or before a justice of the piece to be dealt with according to law..

Notes to the 1967 Provisional Order Confirmation Act.

This only confers powers on London Boroughs in relation to open spaces which they own or have responsibility for management. The rights of course take subject to any third party rights.

Most common land and village green is not in the documented ownership of the local authority and may be in the ownership of 'lords of the manor' or trustees.

Some common land is operated under ancient private acts of parliament and enclosure awards.

As far as greater London is concerned, these 1967 powers predate and run concurrently with the more extensive powers which all districts, counties and unitaries now have under section 123A of the Local Government Act 1972 to dispose of (either on sale or lease) open space which is in their ownership [other than common land or town or village green or greenbelt subject to the restrictions contained in the Green Belt (London and Home Counties) Act 1938, subject to the requirement to advertise the intended disposal or appropriation and after having given due consideration to any representations received in response to such advertisements.

Party Wall etc Act 1996

This legislation is not specific to local authorities but applies when any landowner intends to build any party wall against or astride the boundary with another neighbouring property; or to carry out work on an existing party wall of party structure or building against the party wall or party structure; or to excavate within three metres of a neighbouring building.

The 1996 Act then requires the landowner intending to carry out such works to serve notice on the adjoining owner of such intended works. Then follows a statutory process by which the adjoining owner can either agree or object to the proposed works and with reference to the award of an independent surveyor where the parties cannot agree.

The Act also carries with it power for an owner to serve notice of intention to enter on to the adjoining property to carry out works which have been authorised under the Act.

Note that the term, 'adjoining owner' includes any freeholder or leaseholder except a yearly tenant or a tenancy which is either periodic door for less than the year.

What this means is that there is no statutory requirement to serve notice of intended works on a secure tenant, although, as has already been explained, it is good practice to keep residential tenants involved in the process, to avoid difficulties later.

However the tenant is entitled to be given to notice, in accordance with the provisions of the Act, of any intended entry to their home for the purposes of carrying out works which have been authorized within the terms of the Act.

9 DEVELOPMENT AND COMPULSORY PURCHASE

In this chapter we pull together everything we have learnt so far in previous chapters relating to the drafting of documentation, devolution of title, addressing constitutional and vires issues, and making the best use of the statutory tools which are available to a local authority conveyancer. We will be looking at a complex development proposal where a local authority will be working with a development partner to redevelop a dilapidated housing estate to provide new affordable housing with associated facilities.

We also provide an overview of the compulsory purchase process, as an additional tool in the armoury of the local authority conveyancer. Every new local authority regeneration project begins its life as an idea.

Perhaps it is the subject of an options appraisal, where other options are considered including a 'do nothing' option. But even before any corporate decision has been made to take forward a regeneration project, you may be asked to to carry out a detailed title investigation to assess whether the project-option is even feasible in terms of title constraints.

It is then, only after you have reported back to your corporate client as regards title constraints, that they will be able to make an informed decision on whether to recommend the project to elected-members to make a policy decision and to give the constitutional 'go ahead' to officers to take the project forward.

Because of the statutory right-to-buy, which has existed since the beginning of the 1980s, it is likely that individual houses and flats will have been sold off to council tenants, and will need to be repurchased. Likewise, there may be public utilities crossing through the land which need to be diverted as well as highways to be extinguished.

When it comes to a proposed redevelopment, the title investigation does not only involve an identification and assessment of documented constraints affecting the land but should also suggest practical solutions for dealing with those constraints.

The Next Stage

Once a preliminary assessment of the land title has been carried out, the corporate client will be in a position to work up its development proposals, according to what is feasible for the site and to think about selecting its development partner.

Whilst this book is not primarily written for procurement lawyers, any procurement of a development partner should be guided by the terms of the council's own contract standing orders which, in turn, should be compliant with the current law as it relates to local authority procurement.

The Heads of Terms

The negotiated heads of terms for any complex land-transaction provides the reference point for taking the transaction forward to exchange of contracts and completion.

It is therefore important that the local authority conveyancers who will be taking forward that transaction provide detailed input into the heads of terms, which then becomes an agreed document, though, at this point, not yet contractual he binding

Constitutional Process

It is important that every stage of the transaction is covered by a constitutional approval either in the form of a cabinet or other committee decision or alternatively signed off by a chief officer with the delegated authority to make that decision and that this is evidenced in case of future query.

Most local authority publish their decisions on their website, although some parts of the published decision may be outside of the public domain because of reasons of confidentiality. Like the heads of terms, the conveyancer who will be dealing with the transaction should ideally have input into any committee or delegated reports.

The Document Package

The contractual documentation for a complex redevelopment project, where the council is working with a development partner, will usually comprise a portfolio of documents, at the top of which will be the overarching agreement (often described as the 'Development Agreement'), which then pulls together the subsidiary documentation and the transaction.

It is the development agreement which will detail each stage of the project and specify, 'who does what'.. A development project will usually be in several stages, namely:

First stage:

Most development agreements will contain a raft of contract pre-conditions, which have to be met, to the satisfaction of both parties, before the contract can become 'unconditional'. What this means is that the terms of the contract will be binding on the parties from the date it is signed and dated but that the bulk of the contractual provisions cannot take effect until those pre-conditions have been satisfied. Examples of pre-conditions are:
1. Preliminary site surveys to confirm that the land is suitable for the development proposed.
2. Obtaining a 'satisfactory planning permission' if for the proposed development, in other words, a planning permission which enables the developer to do what it needs to do and is

free from any onerous conditions which would otherwise make the development unviable financially.
3. Repurchase of any third party interests;
4. Resolving any other issues which might otherwise prevent the development being brought to completion.
5. Obtaining any other third party consents, which are required to enable the development to proceed for completion.

There will also be contractual provision enabling either party to bring the contract to an end, before development even starts, if it becomes apparent that the contract-pre-conditions cannot be met to enable a timely development.

Sitting beneath the development agreement will be other supplemental documentation including: template leases or land-transfers; works licences; sstatutory agreements; collateral warranties including, where appropriate, an NHBC or equivalent warranty documentation, where the development includes the provision of housing units.

These supplemental documents will, in the main, not be signed until the development agreement has become unconditional but will exists as pro forma templates attached to the development agreement.

Where the proposed redevelopment will sit beneath the umbrella of a compulsory purchase order, the associated documentation may include a Compulsory Purchase Indemnity Agreement, whereby the local authority will make at the compulsory purchase order at the development partner's request and expense. The final stage occurs after the development agreement has become unconditional and the development itself is being built out to practical completion, possibly against a stage payments made by the local authority to the contractor, based on the value of the work progressed each month.

In many cases, the development partner will not be carrying out the development directly but employing its own building contractor or and have professional team, who will also warrant directly with the local authority.

The what ifs?

Any long-term commercial agreement, particularly relating to the proposed development of land, must cover every potential situation, particularly if things do not go entirely to plan. Suppose planning permission is delayed or refused? Is there a right of appeal? Certainly not where a local authority would be appealing against itself.

What happens if a development partner gets into financial difficulties and cannot progress the development? What if construction is delayed because of inclement weather? What if there are difficulties in obtaining vacant possession of any part of the site, to enable the development to be carried out? What happens if land contamination is discovered or some other physical obstacle threatens to impede the redevelopment, such as the discovery of an underground cellar which no-one previously knew existed?

Should any of these eventualities occur, or anything else which impede development, the development agreement must provide a workable reference point. A well-drawn development agreement should also contain step-in the rights, entitling the council to take over the contract and appoint its own contractors to finish the work if there is serious developer-default.

Construction Documents

In this section we look at some of the main construction documents which sits beneath the development agreement and which can be summarised as follows:

The Building Contract – which is not to be confused with the overarching Development Agreement between the local authority which commissioned the project and its development partner. Whilst the local authority will usually have the right to approve the appointment of the building contractor and the terms of the building contract, it would normally be up to the named developer to make and document that appointment using one of the printed standard-form building contracts (such as JCT – Joint Contracts Tribunal).

Collateral Warranties – These are usually three-party agreements' made between council which has commissioned the project; the principal building contractor and the nominated subcontractor. Under the terms of the Collateral Warranty, the subcontractor will warrant directly with the council, that it will carry out its work to the required standard. There will usually be a separate collateral warranty signed by each consultant or subcontractor who has been commissioned to undertake any part of the project. Counted amongst collateral warranties is the standard NHBC (National House Building Council) 10 the year certificate provided on completion of each new dwelling, or something similar, such as a Premier Guarantee.

Employers Requirements-which list out in great detail the technical output specification for the project and which will be appended to and form part of the development agreement.

Accommodation Schedule, which, in the case of residential developments, will spell out the number and size of individual units, together with those having special features, such as being wheelchair accessible.

Cost Aanalysis-which takes the form of a spreadsheet setting out the itemise cost of the development.

Development Agreement-General Content

The general content of any well-drawn development agreement between a council and its development partner would normally include adequate contractual provision for each of the following:

1. Contract pre-conditions: such as town planning; financial viability; and site surveys, which need to be satisfied before development can even start.

2. Subject to satisfaction of the contract pre-conditions, the developer will be under an obligation to commence construction and complete construction within an agreed timescale, with provisions for extension or force majeur (or unforeseen events which significantly delayed completion of the project and are beyond the control of either party).
3. A change control mechanism-which enables either party to propose changes if to the output-specification with accompanying price-adjustments.
4. Payments obligations on behalf of the local authority commissioning the project, which will tie in to the appended cost schedule.
5. Default provisions, which may include liquidated damages for every week of delay with provisions for termination, as a last resort, if the project cannot be brought to completion either because of the default of either party or for other reasons beyond either party's control. These default provisions may include step-in rights, entitling the council to remove its development partner from the contract and deal directly with sub-contractors or alternatively appoint its own contractors to finish the project.
6. Workable dispute resolution provisions, which enable disputes between the council and its development partner to be resolved quickly and, where possible, without totally destroying the business relationship between the parties.
7. Detailed provisions relating to what documentation is to be handed over to the council by its development partner on completion of the development when it is handed over to the council for occupation, if that is the case.
8. Most public-private development partnerships will include provisions for the transfer of land, either on freehold or on lease.

Compulsory Purchase

Compulsory purchase is a specialist area of law in its own right.

Many larger in-house departments may have a dedicated team of regeneration lawyers. Or such strategic work may be outsourced to a private firm of solicitors who specialise in such work. All we can do in this book is provide an overview of the compulsory purchase process.

Compulsory purchase can relate to the acquisition of a single building or it could extend to the site for a new town. Most compulsory purchase orders are somewhere in between.

Only government departments as well as principal local authorities (being counties, districts or unitaries), as well as certain public utilities, can make compulsory purchase orders. Town and parish councils, being the bottom tier of local government, have no statutory power to make compulsory purchase orders in their own right but can ask their district or unitary council to make a CPO on their behalf.

There are many powers entitling councils to make compulsory purchase orders for specified functions, including education, town planning and housing, but the process for making compulsory purchase orders is the same, as set out in the Compulsory Purchase Act 1965 and the Acquisition of Land Act 1981.

Compensation for land which has been has been acquired pursuant to a CPO, is set out in the Land Compensation Acts of 1961 and 1973. Every step in the CPO process must be absolutely correct or the CPO process will fail. Whilst a CPO will only become legally effective after it has been confirmed by the Secretary of State, an unconfirmed CPO is not without effect, as will be seen in the next chapter when we look at stamp duty land tax reliefs. The stages in any compulsory purchase can be summarised as follows:

1. An initial title investigation to identify who owns what.
2. Identify what land needs to be acquired for the project and, just as importantly, what specific statutory powers should be used to acquire that land or form the basis of a future CPO.
3. A resolution of the council's cabinet or other executive committee, authorising the making of the particular compulsory purchase order and, just as importantly, approving a 'Statement of Reasons', for the making of that order. Note that both the

4. Once an in-principle executive decision has been made to take forward the CPO process, the next task is to commission a detailed land referencing exercise to identify every land or occupational interest which may be affected by the CPO. Even where the legal work is being dealt with in-house, it is common to outsource such land referencing to a specialist land referencing company, such as Terraquest, who will serve statutory notices on everyone believed or suspected of having an interest in land affected by the proposed CPO, so that nothing is a overlooked. As part of that service, the referencing company, will also prepare a schedule of land interests, which will form part of the CPO.

5. On completion of the land referencing exercise and as authorised by the earlier executive decision, the regeneration lawyer is now in a position to make and advertise the CPO for two successive weeks, giving at least 21 days from the date of the first advertisement for the making of our objections. On the same date that the first advertisement appears, a formal written notice of the making of the CPO should be received by everyone whose land interest is directly affected by the CPO, together with a copy of the statement of reasons'. The CPO should also be advertised on the council's own website. During the whole of the objection period, a sealed copy of the CPO should be placed on public deposit for anyone to inspect. Note that a CPO has to be made under seal. The plan also needs to be to the required scale and follow regulatory he conventions as regards delineations and also bear the corporate seal and attestation.

6. As soon as the CPO has been made, a copy of that CPO and the statement of reasons must be sent to the Secretary of State with an application for confirmation. It may be that some objections are addressed directly to the Secretary of State, whilst

other objections may be addressed to the local authority making the order. Either way, copies of those objections must reach the Secretary of State as soon as possible. If no-one affected by the CPO objects to it, or if all objections are withdrawn, the CPO may proceed directly to confirmation or the government department may authorise the originating authority to self-confirm the CPO in the absence of objection. Many objections to CPO are made by public utilities who have apparatus situated under the land affected. Whilst those utilities may have no objection in principle to the proposed CPO, they will make a tactical objection in order to protect their own interests, which may be negotiated away by the local authority offering a replacement Deed of Grant.

7. If an objection is received by someone directly affected by the CPO and that objection is not withdrawn, the likely next step will be the convening of a public inquiry to determine that objection.

8. Once a CPO has been confirmed by the Secretary of State, either in the absence of section or following a public inquiry, the originating authority will be notified of such confirmation and would then need to put in place a second round of statutory advertisement and notifications relating to the confirmed order.

9. The remaining step in the CPO process is for the transfer of title of the lands affected by the CPO, to the local authority and the settlement of compensation claims. The traditional way for an originating authority to acquire title pursuant to a confirmed CPO, is to serve a Notice to Treat on the affected owner followed by a conventional conveyancing transaction to transfer title, as soon as terms are agreed or determined, in default of agreement, by the Upper Tribunal Lands Chamber. The modern way for an originating authority to acquire title following confirmation of its CPO is to make a vesting declaration pursuant to the Vesting Declarations Act 1981, the effect of which is to automatically vest title to all lands affected

by the GVD in the local authority, leaving it to the dispossessed landowners to follow up their claims for compensation which, again, will be referred to the Upper Tribunal in the absence of agreement.

10. When making a CPO for a large development project, it is also good practice to determine what other statutory processes need to be put in hand at the same time, such as for the extinguishment of highway rights which might otherwise impede the proposed development.

10 TAXATION

It is important that any complex conveyancing transaction is as tax-efficient as is possible, particularly as regards the main transaction taxes, which are stamp duty land tax, value added tax and community infrastructure levy. In this section we will review the specific exemptions from SDLT which can assist in reducing the tax burden for local authorities as well as other parties involved in the transaction.

When it comes to value added tax, the main issue is to ensure that any value added tax paid by a party to the transaction is to recoverable as an input.

Whilst it may be good practice to engage a specialist tax adviser (whether internal or external) to ensure that a complex land-transaction is as tax-efficient as possible, it is still important that the conveyancer dealing with a transaction knows enough about the tax implications to ask the right questions; apply that tax advice in structuring of a conveyancing transaction and act as the interface between the tax adviser and the corporate client.

We start with stamp duty land tax, which was originally introduced by the Gordon Brown Labour Government to replace stamp duty on documents which, as the UK's oldest tax, had existed for centuries
. Unless specific exemptions apply, councils will pay Stamp Duty Land Tax on their land purchases.

Stamp Duty rates are progressive, and those local authorities with a housing revenue account, will have to pay the 3% surcharge on residential purchases.

For Treasury purposes, payment of stamp duty land tax by local authorities might be seen as a simple case of money passing from one public sector bank account to another. But the reality is that it potentially sucks money out of any regeneration budget.

From the point of view of the local authority, it is dead money. Like VAT on petrol, it is also a tax-on-tax, in which SDLT is paid not only on the net purchase price but also on any VAT applicable to that purchase price. But SDLT is not the only tax which needs to be factored into regeneration budget.

Even where there is no stamp duty land tax to be paid on a property-acquisition, either because it is below stamp duty thresholds or because one of the statutory reliefs applies, there will still be an obligation to file a stamp duty land tax return (SDLT1) within 14 days from completion of the transaction, unless the value of the transaction does not exceed £40,000. If the return is not filed within deadline, there will be automatic penalties, even if the transaction itself would not otherwise be chargeable to SDLT. Remember also, that even though it is the conveyancer who deals with the submission of the SDLT1, it is the client-officer who takes responsibility for the accuracy of the information contained in it, including to eligibility for any statutory reliefs from SDLT, and who must therefore approve the content of the form before its submission.

The other main property tax is **VAT,** which applies to some property transactions but not others and in different ways.

Dependent on the tax-status of the particular piece of land which is being purchased, VAT can potentially add an additional 20% to the cost of land purchase (as well as the additional SDLT payable on that 20%).

The issue with VAT is not so much whether the tax is triggered by the particular transaction but whether the paying party is VAT registered and therefore able to recover the VAT paid as an input.

A third property tax is **Community Infrastructure Levy,** which is a local tax payable on the implementation of a planning permission. Although these are the main taxes, which are relevant to housing regeneration, the list is not exhaustive.

Other tax issues include: **Capital Gains Tax; Corporation Tax; Income Tax; Council Tax; Business Rates and Capital Allowances**. We now look in a little more detail at each of these property taxes.

Starting with stamp duty land tax, it is important to note the differences in the way residential and non-residential properties (including mixed use) are assessed.

The general rule that SDLT is also paid on the VAT element of a transaction, does not apply to a particular class of commercial transaction where the parties have agreed that it will be classed as the **Transfer of a Business as a Going Concern (or TOGC)**.

An example of a TOGC is an investment sale of an industrial estate where each of the units are rented out as a business. Therefore, where a transaction can be treated as a TOGC, on a VAT opted property, SDLT will only be assessed a on the net purchase price.

This can result in significant SDLT savings on a transaction, if it means that the absence of 20% VAT does not push the value of the transaction above the higher SDLT thresholds.

VAT Notice 700/9 sets out the circumstances which must apply to obtain TOGC relief against SDLT. These include a requirement that, before the transaction completes, the buyer has opted the land for VAT and has notify the seller, before the relevant date, that this option has not been disapplied. For the acquisition of a market rent commercial lease, SDLT will be paid on the capitalised value of the market rental.

What is important for any housing regeneration project is the **SDLT reliefs** which are available. These can be found in official **HMRC Guidance, 'Stamp Duty Land Tax: Relief for Land or Property Transactions** (updated 29th May 2024). Those most applicable to many local authority land transactions, can be summarised as follows:

- *Multiple Dwelling Relief* (MDR), *which* **(up until 1st June 2024**) *applied where a single transaction comprised a number of dwelling houses and which enabled SDLT to be calculated on the average price of* each individual dwelling instead of the cumulative total price of all the dwellings. Notethat MDR has since been abolished for transactions completing after 38 May 2024, save where contracts were exchanged before 6 March, 2024. Even where multiple dwelling relief can no longer apply to a council's bulk purchase of residential dwellings and where the number of units being purchased is at least six or more, alternative relief is available under section 116(7) of the Finance Act 2003, which states, **'Where six or more separate dwellings are the subject of a single transaction involving the transfer of a major interest in, or the grant of a lease over, them, then, for the purposes of this Part as it applies in relation to that transaction, those dwellings are treated as not being residential property'**. In other words, the local authority can then take advantage of the more beneficial rates which apply to the SDLT treatment of non-residential transactions.

- **Compulsory Purchase Relief**, which applies if any property is acquired by a local authority under the umbrella of a compulsory purchase order but only if it is the acquiring authority's intention to transfer the property on to another party for the purpose of redevelopment. Without that forward sale, normal SDLT would be payable on the acquisition. **Compulsory purchase relief is not intended to make the transaction tax free. What it is intended to do is to avoid the double taxation which would otherwise apply on the council's acquisition of the property under the CPO, followed by the development partner's purchase of the same property from the acquiring authority.** Compulsory Purchase Relief can still apply even to a voluntary sale to the acquiring authority under the backdrop of an unconfirmed CPO.

- **Planning Obligation Relief**, which applies where a developer acquires land from a third party on which to build a community facility (such as school) which, on completion of construction, will be transferred to a local authority pursuant to a contractual commitment contained within a planning obligation made pursuant to **Section 106 Town and Country Planning Act 1990**. Like compulsory purchase relief, the purpose of this exemption this to avoid double taxation on the developer's acquisition of the Section 106 land from the third party – and again when the local authority takes an onward transfer of the completed school.

- ***Transfer of Property between companies*** *which are members of the same group when the transaction takes place.*
- ***Charity Relief,*** *which applies when a charity buys land and property for charitable purposes.*
- ***Registered Social Landlord Relief,*** *which applies where an RSL buys land and property where* **any** *of the following conditions are met:*
  a) *Most of the board members of the RSL are tenants living in properties rented from the RSL;*
  b) *The* **seller** *of the property is a 'qualifying body', such as a local authority; or*
  c) *A public subsidy funds the sale. Note: that although a local housing authority can now be regarded as an RSL, this relief will only be available where the transaction is at least part-funded by any government grant. For London Boroughs, this will mean funding provided by the GLA.*

SDLTM04015 - Scope: How much is chargeable: Sale of land with associated construction contract - Para 10 Schedule 4 Finance Act 2003

This paragraph deals with determining the chargeable consideration for stamp duty land tax purposes where the V (the vendor) agrees to sell land to the P (purchaser) and V also agrees to carry out work, commonly works of construction, improvement or repair, on the land sold.

HMRC view is that the decision in Prudential Assurance Co Ltd v IRC [1992] STC 863 applies for the purposes of Stamp Duty Land Tax (SDLT) as it did for stamp duty. This is because the basis of the decision was the identification of the subject matter of the transaction and this is as relevant for SDLT as it is for stamp duty.

The identification of the subject matter of the transaction must have regard to the commercial substance of the transaction.

A common example is where land is transferred by V to P and at that date the work on the land either has not started or is incomplete.

In this case the subject matter of the land transaction will normally be the land in its condition at the date of transfer.

In other words the consideration for SDLT purposes will, subject to apportionment as mentioned below, be the consideration attributable to the land, together with the consideration attributable to the work already carried out on the land at the date of transfer.

There may be cases however where the agreement for the sale of the land is so interlocked with the agreement for works that it is not capable of independent completion.

This may occur in particular if the agreements provide that if default occurs on one agreement the other is not enforceable.

In such a case the subject matter of the land transaction will be the land with the works completed, so that the chargeable consideration will be the aggregate consideration.

Where the sale of land and the construction, etc, contract are in substance one bargain, as they were in the Prudential case, there must be a just and reasonable apportionment of the total consideration given for all elements of the bargain in order to arrive at the chargeable consideration for SDLT purposes.

Note to SDLTM04015. When a local authority acquires land in the course of development, the first question is whether the transaction, as a whole, would qualify for any of the statutory reliefs against Stamp Duty Land Tax as listed above. If 100% relief can be obtained, the structuring of the transaction is not so much an issue. However where SDLT is payable on the local authority purchase, the way the transaction is structured can significantly affect its treatment for SDLT, particularly where development is involved. If the local authority does not take ownership of the development until the development itself is substantially completed, then SDLT will be payable on the as-built development. However if the land can be acquired before development commences as a stand-alone transaction, then SDLT will only be paid on the land-price and the subsequent development of that land on behalf of the local authority will need to be the subject of a separate stand alone construction contract. What is important in those circumstances is that there is no contractual inter-dependency in the terms of the two contracts, even if they are entered into back-to-back. Many local authority development agreements, whether involving an acquisition by the local authority or transfer of an estate from the local authority to a third party, refer to 'Golden Brick' as the trigger points for completion of the sale. The significance of the term 'golden brick' and its wider tax-implications are explained in greater detail later in this chapter. For the moment, we refer only to 'Golden Brick' as a common trigger point for completion of sales and purchases, which means that, for the purposes of the SDLT, the value of the land-transaction will be assessed at the point the construction has progressed to 'golden brick', which is normally taken to be one layer of construction above foundation level.

Practical note when paying SDLT. A challenge for any local authority conveyancer, having a uploaded the SDLT1 on to the HMRC website if, is to ensure that any resulting SDLT due on the transaction is paid within the required 14 days, to avoid penalties or interest. Just as important is the need to ensure that any payment of SDLT put through to HMRC Shipley by the council's finance team can be easily traced by HMRC and matched to the particular transaction. However this can only happen if the SDLT on a particular transaction is put through as a single payment and is correctly referenced by the UTRN, which will be generated automatically when the SDLT5 is issued. Anything else will lead to extensive and tiresome follow-up correspondence, when you receive a letter from the HMRC querying why the tax is not been paid.

Value Added Tax Look at any conveyancing document pre-1990 and it is unlikely that you'll see any reference to VAT. That's because VAT had never applied to property transactions, even though VAT had been introduced almost twenty years before, to replace purchase tax. So it was taken for granted that VAT would never apply. Land sales were classed within VAT legislation as 'exempt'. But all that changed at the beginning of the 1990s, when the UK government became obliged by EU law to introduce a VAT regime for land transactions. What was originally intended to be 'light touch' has become a complicated tax-structure which is applied piecemeal in the sense that the tax-treatment is applied differently according to the particular class of property-transaction: with some transactions being classed as 'exempt'; others as zero rated; and with a third category taxed at the full 20% rate. And as we have already seen, the imposition of 20% standard rate VAT on a land acquisition translates into an increase of at least 20% on the SDLT bill (unless the transaction can be classed as a TOGC). There is a further complication in that in some cases landowners can 'opt' to make their land VAT-taxable, even when it might otherwise be classed as 'exempt'. So why would you want to waive that tax-exemption? Perhaps as a result of detailed tax advice (see below) or the ability to be able to recover the VAT input on construction and related development costs. The default positions of different types of property transaction can be summarised as follows:

- *Sales of residential accommodation are technically taxable but classed as 'Zero Rated' (which is why there is no VAT to pay on the purchase or rent of someone 's home). 'Zero Rating' has an advantage over 'Exempt' when it comes to recovery of VAT paid out.*
- *A freehold sale of commercial new-build (within the first three years after construction) is compulsory rated at 20%;*
- *For other commercial transactions (Including the grant of leases), whether or not VAT is charged on the rent or sale price depends upon whether the seller (or a previous owner) has notified HMRC of an* **'option to tax'**. *Unless that option has been expressly exercised at sometime in the past, the default position remains that the transaction is 'VAT Exempt'.*

VAT Notice 742: Land and Property (Published 29th May 2012) sets out in detail the particular types of land transaction to which a liability for VAT will arise, whether as standard or through exercise of an option.

For example a lease or licence of garaging or parking spaces will normally be standard rated unless incidental to some other use. If the rules for charging or not-charging VAT on property transactions are complex, the rules for recovering paid VAT are even more so.

The general rule is that an organisation which is registered for VAT and makes taxable supplies of goods and services, can recover any VAT which it has had to pay out on its own purchases, as an input.

Conversely an organisation which makes only exempt supplies, such as a housing association renting out homes, cannot recover its VAT. It is why it will rarely be viable for a housing association to purchase land on which there has been an option to tax.

As local authorities provide a mixture of business; non-business and exempt supplies, the rules relating to the recovery of VAT are particularly complex.

Official guidance is provided by **VAT Notice 749: Local Authorities and Similar Bodies** (updated 8th February 2016), which helps local authorities and other public bodies decide which activities are business or non-business.

When commissioning major construction projects, local authorities must take particular care to ensure that any transactions related to that project are structured in a way which does not prejudice recovery of VAT on those construction costs.

Golden Brick is often the optimum stage for completion of a transfer of land, in residential construction, to take place, particularly where the buyer is a registered social landlord and which is unable to recover its VAT on its land purchase and related construction costs as an input.

Before golden brick has occurred, the undeveloped land will either be regarded for the purposes of value added tax as 'exempt' or 'standard rated'. However many housebuilders wanting to acquire land for development will opt to 'standard rate' the land for VAT so that it can recover VAT on its construction cost.

Golden brick is then the point in construction at which HMRC will recognise that the residential construction is sufficiently underway for the development to become zero rated for VAT.

It would therefore make no sense for an RSL to complete its purchase of a standard rated land before Golden Brick, at which point, the VAT liability on the land value would revert to zero. As previously stated, golden brick is usually taken to mean completion of the first layer of construction above foundation level.

Completion of the purchase at golden brick also means that, for the purposes of SDLT, the transaction would be valued at its golden brick price, which would only be a fraction of the price payable if the purchase delayed until completion of the development itself.

Note: that where a land-sale is standard rated, it is important that the seller provides a VAT invoice for the purchase money when the transaction completes, so that the buyer can recover the VAT as an input, where it is possible to do so.

The same will apply where a deposit is paid on exchange of contracts. Where on any transaction, a seller, or a predecessor of the seller, has opted to standard-rate land for the purposes of the VAT, it is important that evidence of that option to tax is provided, for the record.

Community Infrastructure Levy

Community Infrastructure Levy (or CIL) was introduced in the final years of the Blair/Brown Government in their **Planning Act 2008** and adopted by the incoming Coalition Government in its **Community Infrastructure Levy Regulations 2010** as amended.

It was introduced with the intention of replacing the financial contributions towards infrastructure improvements which would otherwise have had to be contained in Section 106 Planning Obligations.

It is a tariff based system designed to cover the costs of all local infrastructure needs. It requires local planning authorities (known as 'charging authorities') to produce '**Charging Schedules'** setting out their levy rates for different types of development. Here is a summary of how the CIL Regime works:

- *Under the 2010 Regulations a potential liability for CIL arises on a grant of planning permission for the construction of any new residential house or flat (of any size) or other development exceeding 100 Square Metres floor area (but not on residential extensions).*
- *A liability for CIL can only arise where the local planning authority has published a Charging Schedule within the Regulations. That Charging Schedule will apply different rates per square metre for different types of residential or commercial development. The money raised through a Charging Schedule must have a direct link to the expenditure required to pay for infrastructure improvements falling on the public purse and which are required to accommodate new developments.*

- *On the grant of a new planning permission, the Charging Authority (which is the local planning authority) will issue a **Liability Notice** in respect of the CIL which will be due in respect of that particular development. However the obligation to pay that CIL will not actually arise until development is formally commenced. Developers are under a legal obligation to notify the Charging Authority when development is about to start and provide details of the person who has accepted responsibility for payment of the CIL. If that preliminary notice is not given to the charging authority, the obligation to pay CIL will have been triggered by the start of development itself, in which case the Charging Authority will make its own assessment of whom is responsible for payment in accordance with the default provisions set out in the regulations. Once issued, a Liability Notice is registered as a Local Land Charge, which will be removed from the register on payment of the CIL.*
- *The 2010 Regulations exempt charities from any requirement to pay CIL for developments on their own land which will be used for charitable purposes. There is also a **Social Housing Relief**, which applies to developments by registered providers and local authorities and which is calculated according to complex formulae. This is perhaps the most important relief, at least as regards the development of land as affordable housing, and we now look at this in a little more detail.*

To qualify for mandatory social housing relief the claimant must have a material interest in the relevant land and have assumed liability to pay the levy for the whole of the chargeable development.

The relief applies to new social rent, affordable rent and intermediate rent dwellings provided by a local authority or private registered provider and shared ownership dwellings. It can also apply to discounted rental property provided by other bodies.

Mandatory social housing relief can also benefit other dwellings where first or subsequent sales will be priced at no more than 70% of market value, where this is the subject of a section 106 planning obligation to ensure that subsequent sales will not be at more than 70% of current value.

A charging authority may also offer discretionary RSL relief for dwellings sold at not more than 80% of market value, subject to specific criteria. For all developments affected by any charge to community infrastructure levy, charging authorities expect developers, landowners or other interested parties, to assume liability for the tax in good time. Any claim for RSL or Charity relief against the community infrastructure levy which would otherwise fall due, must be formally submitted using **Form 10 "Charitable and/or Social Housing Relief",** before development commences.

.Like SDLT, a local authority's payment of CIL on a development project is a case of money being taken out of one public purse and being transferred to another. Only more so, because in many cases it will be the same local authority which is paying the CIL as is receiving it but in different budgets. But again, it sucks money out of the regeneration pot. For any regeneration project, it is therefore important at the outset:

- To identify what property taxes are likely to be involved and to budget for them; and
- To structure the transaction (or multiple transactions) in the way which is considered most tax efficient. For the largest projects this will inevitably involve commissioning external tax advice from accountancy firms such as Price Waterhouse Cooper on exactly how the transactions should best be structured.

INDEX

allotment land, **114, 115**
anti-money-laundering, **37, 38, 40, 53, 58**
appropriation, **94, 98, 105, 111, 114, 115, 116, 117, 118, 136, 138, 139, 157**
auction sale, **134**
Best Value, **6, 33, 34, 36, 37**
charity, **15, 17, 68, 174**
CIPFA, **34, 35**
client account, **19, 23, 40, 74, 122, 123**
Code for Completion by Post, **20, 38, 120, 122, 123, 124**
Code of Conduct, **21, 27, 29, 30**
Collateral Warranty, **164**
company, **2, 3, 5, 15, 16, 29, 53, 63, 65, 66, 67, 72, 73, 76, 77, 78, 91, 99, 112, 131, 133, 134, 167**
compulsory competitive tendering, **5, 6, 32, 33**
Compulsory Purchase, **139, 162, 166, 173**
conflict of interest, **29, 61, 65**
constitution, **66, 67, 68, 106, 132, 133**
construction, **128, 163, 165, 174, 175, 176, 177, 178, 179, 180**
continuous professional development, **12, 55**
Court of Protection, **17, 18, 68**
covenants, **2, 110, 113, 126, 127, 131, 143, 144, 145, 146, 149, 150, 153**
Data Protection, **30**
deposit, **18, 19, 54, 75, 77, 121, 122, 124, 125, 135, 168, 179**

Deputyship, **17, 18**
development, **3, 55, 57, 65, 79, 87, 89, 91, 97, 98, 99, 103, 104, 109, 110, 126, 130, 136, 137, 139, 140, 141, 142, 143, 146, 148, 150, 152, 153, 159, 160, 161, 162, 163, 164, 165, 166, 169, 173, 175, 177, 179, 180, 181**
devolution of title, **2, 85, 159**
digital registration, **46, 79, 80**
elected member, **15**
execution of documents, **132**
Freedom of Information, **31, 32**
general consent, **99, 100, 105, 108, 110, 117, 126**
golden brick, **176, 178, 179**
Greater London, **78, 85, 86, 87, 88, 89, 128, 130, 144, 150, 154**
greenbelt, **110, 111, 112, 113, 114, 116, 157**
heads of terms, **61, 69, 71, 80, 81, 160, 161**
HMRC, **172, 174, 176, 177, 179**
Housing Revenue Account, **94**
insurance, **25, 26, 42**
Land Registry, **32, 53, 56, 68, 73, 79, 84, 87, 89, 90, 91, 93, 126, 131, 133, 134**
Law Society Practice Note, **9, 21**
local land charge, **17, 76, 78, 83, 128, 129, 130, 131, 132, 144, 146, 149, 152**
London County Council, **85, 112, 113, 114**
management, **2, 20, 28, 30, 33, 35, 36, 39, 42, 45, 47, 48, 49, 50, 62, 63, 65, 66, 80, 85, 109,**

154, 156
Middlesex County Council, 85, 89, 93
mortgage, 16, 17, 20, 54, 75, 76, 77, 78, 123, 131, 145, 146
Occupational interests, 138
open space, 97, 98, 102, 109, 113, 116, 118, 154, 155, 156, 157
overriding rights, 128, 141
party wall, 142, 157
planning obligation, 130, 150, 151, 152, 153, 174, 181
practising certificate, 10, 11, 12, 57, 73
public rights of way, 143
public trust, 9, 97, 109, 110, 116
public utility, 140
registration, 51, 61, 62, 67, 73, 77, 79, 80, 82, 84, 85, 89, 90, 91, 93, 128, 130, 131, 133, 146, 149
reliefs, 167, 171, 172, 176
restriction, 93, 110, 113, 114, 117, 127, 137, 139, 151, 153
School Playing Fields, 105
SDLT, 170, 171, 172, 173, 175, 176, 177, 179, 181
stamp duty land tax, 62, 80, 82, 167, 170, 171, 172, 174
Standard Commercial Property Conditions, 19, 20, 74, 120
Standard Conditions of Sale, 19, 20, 74, 120, 121, 123, 125
statutory agreement, 132, 149
telecommunications rights, 140
Third Party Managed Accounts, 22
time-charging, 33, 44, 45
TOGC, 172, 177
Transparency Rules, 24, 44
undertake, 10, 19, 20, 24, 39, 58, 86, 102, 120, 124, 125, 164
undertaking, 19, 54, 75, 77, 106, 123, 124, 125, 144, 145, 148
unrepresented, 52, 53, 54, 55
value added tax, 170, 179

TABLE OF REFERENCES

Acquisition of Land Act 1981..161
Community Infrastructure Levy 166, 174
Contracts (Rights of Third Parties) Act 1999 149
Economic Crime (Transparency and Enforcement) Act............................72
General Consent for the Disposal of Land..93
Greater London Council (General Powers) Act 1974....................... 124, 140
Green Belt (London and Home Counties) Act 1938. 107
Housing Act 1985...passim
Housing and Planning Act Act 2016 132
Law of Property Act 77, 128
Local Authorities (England)(Property etc)Order 1973...............................85
Local Authorities (Goods and Services)(Public Bodies) Order....................14
Local Government (Miscellaneous Provisions) Act 1982.... **125, 127, 139, 142**
Local Government Act 1972 ....passim
Local Government and Housing Act 1989 .... **15, 66**
Local Government and Public Involvement to Health Act 2007..................84
Local Government Reorganisation (Property etc) Order (No 2)1986 86
Local Government Reorganisation (Property etc) Order 1986 86
Localism Act 2011... **7, 16, 65**
London Authorities (Property etc) Order 1964...85
Michael Cantrell V Wycombe District Council, [2008] EWCA Civ 866 145
Ministry of Housing and Local Government Provisional Order Confirmation
149
Open Spaces Act 1906...passim
Overseas Investment Services Ltd. V Simcobuild Construction Ltd and
 Swansea City Council, 1995 70 PandCR 322..145
Public Health Act **95, 106, 111, 144**
R *(on the application of Day) (Appellant) v Shropshire Council (Respondent) [2023]*
 UKSC 8,..95
Regina v Secretary of State for the Environment, Transport and the Regions (Appellant)
 and others ex parte O'Byrne (respondent) [2003] 1 All ER 15,........................109
School standards and Framework Act 1998..102
Section 609 Housing Act 1985 145

Solicitors Accounts Rules 22
Solicitors Act 1974 10
the Buckinghamshire (Structural Changes)Order 84
The Local Authorities (Companies) Order 16
The Local Government Act 1993 16
Town and Country Planning Act 1990 .... passim
Tulk v Moxhay, 1848 140
Waste Regulation and Disposal Authorities Order 1985 86

ABOUT THE AUTHOR

Charles Ward is a UK registered solicitor and legal writer who writes from his own many years experience in managing conveyancing teams in the London Boroughs of Sutton and Harrow. He is also Company Solicitor for the Institute of Cemetery and Crematorium Management.

www.ingramcontent.com/pod-product-compliance
Lightning Source LLC
Chambersburg PA
CBHW071052240526
45471CB00015B/1710